Using Sources Effectively

Strengthening Your Writing and Avoiding Plagiarism

Second Edition

Robert A. Harris

 Pyrczak Publishing
P.O. Box 250430 • Glendale, CA 91225

"Pyrczak Publishing" is an imprint of Fred Pyrczak, Publisher, A California Corporation.

Project Director: Monica Lopez.

Editorial assistance provided by Brenda Koplin, Sharon Young, Kenneth Ornburn, Cheryl Alcorn, Randall R. Bruce, and Erica Simmons.

Cover design by Robert Kibler and Larry Nichols.

Printed in the United States of America by Malloy, Inc.

ISBN 1-884585-57-4

Contents

Notes

Introduction to the Second Edition

This book is designed to assist you, the writer of a research paper, with practical and effective strategies for incorporating sources into your work. In the chapters that follow, you will learn how the skillful use of sources adds strength to your argument and interest to your writing. You will also learn what you need to know to avoid plagiarism as you bring source material into your research paper. The book includes many examples and ideas to help you apply the strategies and to make your writing especially good.

Overview of the book.

Chapter 1: The Importance of Using Sources Effectively.

This chapter discusses the purposes behind bringing sources into your writing and how the skillful use of quotations, summaries, and paraphrases can give your writing both power and sparkle. By reading this chapter, you should come to view the research process and the use of research materials as an opportunity to enrich your own thinking and provide punch to the arguments you present.

Chapter 2: Avoiding Plagiarism.

This chapter provides practical instruction about what does and does not constitute plagiarism. You may be one of the many students who never received formal instruction about plagiarism and how to incorporate sources appropriately. This chapter defines the issues and clarifies some possible misconceptions in order to help you avoid unintentional plagiarism. It also tells you how to protect yourself from a false charge of plagiarism.

Chapter 3: Selecting Sources.

This chapter covers the selection of sources and describes the various kinds of source material you will find. Some ideas are included for evaluating the quality of the sources you have located, together with advice about handling sources that disagree or conflict with one another or with the central idea you are presenting in your paper.

Chapter 4: Working with Sources.

Through examples, this chapter shows you how to work with your source material and covers the various methods of preparing your sources for incorporation into your paper. Advice is offered about deciding whether to quote, summarize, or paraphrase, and how to preserve the author's intended meaning.

Chapter 5: Putting It Together.

This chapter provides strategies and examples to help you build sources into a paper: introductory methods and styles, the use of appropriate phrases and verbs to help direct your reader, and how to punctuate your quotations accurately.

Chapter 6: Effective Use.

This chapter goes beyond mere compliance with the rules of source use and discusses how to use sources in a powerful and effective way. By employing some of the practical ideas in this chapter, you will be able to write much more vibrant and successful research papers.

Appendix A: Polishing Your Prose.

This appendix provides half a dozen short instructional reminders about grammar, mechanics, and punctuation that writers of research papers often find troublesome. The advice comes from a professor who has been teaching students the process of writing a research paper for more than 25 years. The benefit to you is that the reminders chosen for your attention are based on long experience. One of the secrets of writing instruction is that relatively few error patterns account for a large proportion of the errors in most student writing. If you master the material presented in this appendix, you will most likely have substantially improved the accuracy of your writing.

Appendix B: Citation Examples.

This appendix provides examples of citations for APA References pages and MLA Works Cited pages.

New to the second edition.

This edition has more exercises, including a True-False quiz at the end of each chapter. The mechanics and grammar reviews have been moved to Appendix A, Polishing Your Prose, which includes exercises. In the main text, a section has been added to show how to mark the boundaries for non-text information such as tables and drawings (Chapter 5, Section 5.1.5), and a section is now included on using Internet sources (Chapter 3, Section 3.3). Other improvements include information about plagiarism and copyright infringement, the overuse of tutors, and the benefits of using reference librarians. Clarifications have been made throughout.

Citation and bibliography style.

The examples in the book are presented in both APA and MLA citation styles, though the book should be a useful resource regardless of the particular style of citation and bibliography you use, whether APA, MLA, CBE, Chicago, Turabian, ASA, or some other. APA style follows that of the fifth edition of the *Publication Manual of the American Psychological Association* (2001), and MLA style follows that in the sixth edition of the *MLA Handbook for Writers of Research Papers* (Gibaldi, 2003). The References page near the end of the book follows APA style.

Acknowledgments.

Thanks to Fred Pyrczak, my acquisition editor and publisher, for his continued support for the project and for his helpful comments on the drafts.

Robert A. Harris
Tustin, California

1
The Importance of
Using Sources Effectively

The mind is but a barren soil; a soil which is soon exhausted, and will produce no crop, or only one, unless it be continually fertilized and enriched with foreign matter.
  —Sir Joshua Reynolds

The overall goal of this book is to help you write better research papers, principally by incorporating sources into your work more effectively and accurately. However, a preliminary question may have arisen in your mind: Why do you have to do a research paper anyway? Why do instructors assign them? This chapter will provide you with some answers by discussing the benefits of writing a research paper.

- ◆ Writing a research paper helps to improve your writing skills.
- ◆ Researching brings you new ideas and perspectives.
- ◆ Using sources in a paper adds strength, interest, and context to your argument.
- ◆ Citing sources aids your reader and helps you to avoid plagiarism.
- ◆ Writing with sources develops your thinking and analysis skills.

1.1 Why do research?

Writing—especially research-based writing—is one of the most amazing opportunities you will have in your educational experience. By improving your ability to frame a research problem, locate relevant sources, work with those sources, and write a persuasive paper based on them, you will be developing a host of skills that will serve you well for the rest of your life. Just as swimming is said to be such good exercise because it uses so many different muscles, research-based writing is excellent mental exercise because it develops your skills not just in writing, but in creativity, problem solving, and thinking.

1.1.1 Writing is a thinking process.

It has been said that we really do not know what we think about something until we write about it. Writing requires a deeper and more careful thought process than does speaking or even meditating about a topic. By writing down your ideas, you clarify them to yourself or even discover them. More than one student has remarked, "I never knew I thought that," after writing an essay. Writing, then, is an opportunity to strengthen your thinking ability and to extend your mind, to gain a wider view of a subject, to find personal engagement with the world of ideas, even to make the unknown interesting.

When you work with sources, you learn better how to analyze them, how to evaluate the strength of their arguments, and how to fit them together with other sources that may disagree. The process of writing a paper based on research materials broadens your

1

understanding of how information is used and makes you more careful about accepting unsupported claims.

1.1.2 Writing is a learning process.

Writing is a natural, inseparable part of learning, providing clarity to thinking and solidity to knowing. Writing involves the collection and organization of ideas and thoughts, of analysis, of comparing and contrasting conflicting claims. All of these activities help you learn about a subject. Where before you may have believed that some fact had been clearly established, you discover by researching and writing about it that there are complications to the supposed fact or even more credible alternative explanations of the data behind it.

The act of wide reading, whether in an area of controversy or not, will help you add to your general database of knowledge and your understanding of the world. When you write a paper that synthesizes your reading, you will learn even more about your topic as you sort out the better arguments from the weaker ones. You will also view the world with more understanding as you gain knowledge. As the proverb says, "The more you know, the better you can see."

1.1.3 Writing develops lifelong skills.

The simple truth is this: As an educated person in an ever-more information-driven world, you will be writing for the rest of your life. By developing your writing now, you will acquire the skills you need to work effectively in the future. Whatever form your writing eventually takes—whether keyboard, dictation, or a new mind-reading software application—you will need to know how to use all the skills of writing. Thinking, analyzing, organizing, reasoning, using examples—all these and many other skills are the ones that will allow you not just to survive but to flourish.

Writing a research paper also gives you practice in making a subject interesting. In your future writing career, not every topic you are handed will be of interest to you. The subject may not even be immediately interesting to the targeted readers. It is important, then, for you to develop the ability to make a subject interesting both to yourself and to your readers. The more practice you have doing this now, the better you will become at it and the more you will be able to enjoy writing on any topic.

1.1.4 Writing allows you to contribute to the great conversation.

Writing represents mental work (creative, analytic, persuasive, or some other kind) put down in a fixed form so that others can access it at any time and make use of it. Many readers make use of others' writing simply as a means of learning, but many others use writing as building blocks for further knowledge and for their own writing and thinking. This has been true for thousands of years. As the saying goes, "We stand on the shoulders of giants." Every writer makes use of the work of previous writers, building on thinking and discoveries that have gone before.

Increasingly today, moreover, many writers are building their ideas together. Many corporations are developing knowledge-sharing cultures, where employees can use each other's ideas either by direct collaboration or through the use of knowledge management databases. Developing your writing skills empowers you to take a significant place in this creating and sharing of knowledge. The better writer you become, the better writing partner you will be.

1.2 Why use sources in papers?

Understanding the purpose of using sources in papers should result in better papers. Students who believe that sources serve no purpose other than to decorate or lengthen a paper are more likely to insert long quotations without taking much care to build them into the overall presentation. The result of such a practice is, at best, padding and, at worst, a disjointed collage. Sources serve a number of important functions in a paper, both as part of, and in addition to, the requirement that the paper be based on research.

1.2.1 Research sources provide context.

Suppose you walk up to two strangers and ask them, "What do you put on your strawberries?" One of them says, "Sugar," and the other says, "Cow manure." How are you to understand this discrepancy? If you think for a moment, you will see that context is crucial to interpretation—a proper understanding of events and thought processes requires knowledge of the surrounding information environment. In this case, one of the strangers puts sugar on the strawberries on the breakfast table, while the other puts cow manure on the strawberries (to fertilize them) in the patch out behind the house.

Similarly, when a scholarly paper describes, analyzes, reports, or argues some point, it does not do so in a vacuum. The topic has almost certainly been treated before, experiments may have been conducted, and other interpretations may have already been made. A first function of the use of sources, then, is to provide background information. An overview, the historical context (which may influence meaning as much as the context of the strawberry comments above), a starting point such as the definition of key concepts—these can all be provided by making use of appropriate sources. In many scholarly projects, a review of the literature is a required first part to provide a history of progress in the field, information relating to the topic, a technical context, or other background for the new material to be presented.

1.2.2 Sources strengthen your argument.

One of the myths surrounding research-based writing seems to be that citing sources is a necessary evil, an unfortunate concession required by the rules of composition for giving away credit for ideas. In fact, quite the contrary is true. Using and citing sources actually strengthens your writing in the eyes of your reader, for it demonstrates that you have performed research and have integrated the findings and ideas of others into your own argument.

First, quoting or referring to sources and then discussing them demonstrates that you are aware of other writers' positions on the topic. You are not writing in an intellectual vacuum or off the top of your head, but you have included the ideas of others in the formulation of your own thinking. Next, using sources demonstrates that your ideas have support. Writers whose ideas parallel your argument add major timber to the intellectual house you are building for your reader. Corroboration of thinking or argument, additional facts or evidence from a third party, and the information of experts all provide powerful support to your position. Finally, using and citing sources demonstrates that you can think and argue along with scholars and other professionals and that you are able to interact with the ideas connected to your subject. Your paper's sources, then, far from being a negative, provide positive evidence for your reader about your writing and thinking ability as well as your resourcefulness.

1.2.3 Sources add interest to your paper.

As you do your research, you will discover that sources provide much more than factual information or good analysis. Sources often contain stories, personal experiences, unique data, experimental results, or other items that will add greatly to the interest of your paper. One reason to quote rather than summarize or paraphrase a source is that often the author of the source text has an interesting, colorful, or compelling way of writing. A particular sentence or even a phrase may give just the direct and clear expression of an idea that you need. Even if the source's words are not quotable, you might make the information interesting through an appropriate summary or paraphrase.

1.2.4 Sources provide you with new ideas.

As the epigraph at the beginning of this chapter indicates, our minds need the fertilizer of new ideas if we are to be consistently productive in our intellectual lives. Another critical use of sources, then, is that they enrich your mind with new ideas, give you "food for thought," and allow you to compare several different ways of thinking about an issue. Even if all of the research you discover generally agrees with the position you are taking (and that is not likely), you will still be able to refine your own thinking by discovering the various ways of conceptualizing a given idea. More likely, you will encounter ideas and arguments you have never thought of before, providing you with the opportunity to extend your thinking. You may ultimately alter or even reject the original idea you located in your research because sources have suggested a new direction or a new interpretation that is more useful in your argument. (If you should ever develop a love for classical writers such as Plato and Aristotle, you will discover that they are famous not because they are right about everything but because, when they are wrong, they are wrong in very interesting and provocative ways. They make us think.)

1.2.5 Sources reveal controversies.

You know the saying, "There are two sides to every argument," meaning that every position has its pros and cons. Even this saying has two sides to it. One side claims that the saying is correct. The other side claims that it is not correct because there are almost never only two sides to a given position: Most areas of controversy have several different sides. A benefit of research and the use of your results is to expose the areas of controversy. By pointing out ideas that conflict with your position and by responding reasonably to those who disagree with your argument, you demonstrate first that you are aware of the opposition and that there is a reasonable response to it, and second that your conclusions are based on a full contemplation of all the evidence, not just on that which agrees with the case you are presenting.

Imagine reading a paper about a controversial issue that completely ignores some strong opposing arguments you have heard elsewhere. What do you think of the paper and its writer? Is the writer simply unaware of the other arguments, and hence has based the paper on partial knowledge? Or is the writer aware of them but has decided not to mention them because there is no adequate response? In blunt terms, is the writer ignorant or dishonest?

See Chapter 3 for information about how to incorporate conflicting sources into your papers.

1.2.6 Sources help you understand how reasoned argument works.

The more you work with sources for your research papers, the more information literate you will become. Information literacy is usually defined as the ability to locate, evaluate, and use information appropriately. But the term goes beyond these practices to include an awareness of how information itself works. Specifically, you will discover how a credible argument is assembled, what kind of evidence needs to be brought to bear, how generalizations are formed from experimental samples, and so forth. You will also learn about the role of assumptions, interpretations, and even biases in arguments. (For example, the first time you locate two books each claiming to prove beyond a doubt exactly the opposite conclusion about a controversial subject, you begin to understand much about the world of books and arguments.) Many issues are still unsettled and in flux, and your research will help you become mindful of this.

1.3 Why cite them all?

As you will read again in coming chapters, you must cite the source of each idea or item of information you use, whether you quote, paraphrase, summarize, or merely refer to it. There are several good reasons for this rule.

1.3.1 Cite to help your reader.

The primary reason for citing each use of an external source or idea is to provide a path for your reader to follow in the event he or she is interested in further reading. Imagine your reader encountering one of your quotations or a summary of a study and thinking, "That's really interesting. I'd like to read the whole article." Your citation makes exactly that possible. You are providing a courtesy to your reader. Alternatively, instead of interest, you may have inspired indignation in your reader: "How can Jones make that claim?" your reader may demand. Your citation allows your reader to locate the article or book and read the claim in its context.

For most of your academic papers, your instructor will be your immediate, if not your only, reader. Citations perform the same courtesy here. If your instructor becomes interested (or indignant) after reading one of your sources, he or she can go directly to the source for a look. A look at some of your sources will also help your instructor determine how effectively and accurately you are using research material. Your instructor's comments, based on this determination, will help you write better. In these cases, citing sources helps you, too.

1.3.2 Cite to show respect for fellow knowledge workers.

At this point in your life, you may not be thinking of yourself as a knowledge worker, either present or future. Yet that is just what you are likely to be. The industrial age has passed, and we now live in an information age where processing information and creating knowledge out of it are major tasks of most educated workers. Just as you would not want others to take and use your ideas or writing without crediting you, you should not take the ideas or writing of others without crediting them. It is a matter of respect.

As mentioned in Section 1.1.4 above, more and more knowledge is being created through collaboration with others. A key to the willingness of others to collaborate is the

5

feeling that their intellectual property (their words and ideas) will be duly respected and credited. Those who believe that their ideas will be stolen are not likely to share them.

1.3.3 Cite to avoid plagiarism.

A fundamental requirement of academic work is that you clearly distinguish your words and ideas from those of the sources you use. Citation provides the basic mechanism of distinction. A substantial amount of plagiarism is committed unintentionally, simply because the writer did not know the rules or forms of citation. Yet the penalty for such behavior is often severe because plagiarism is considered one of the most serious forms of academic dishonesty. Therefore, out of self-interest and self-protection, you want to be sure to cite your sources. (Plagiarism and the requirements for citation to avoid it are discussed in detail in the next chapter.)

1.4 Are sources the whole idea?

At least a few students approach research paper assignments with the belief that their own ideas do not count: They think a research paper is to be filled with sources elegantly strung together. These students seem to fear they will be graded down if even one of their own thoughts gets in the way of the sources. This idea is wrong, incorrect, and not true.

1.4.1 Your thinking is the star.

You will recall from Section 1.2.2 above that sources were said to support your thinking. Think of your research paper as a major motion picture. Your thinking, perhaps your central idea, is the star, while the sources you use are the supporting cast. The most important part of a research paper is not the sources themselves but what you do with them. You should use sources to support your own line of argument, your own conclusions, your own ideas. This is your paper we are talking about, not an extended summary of other papers. You are not writing *Bartlett's Familiar Quotations*: That has already been done.

Another way of thinking about your use of sources is to say that just as you should honor the thinking of others by citing their ideas, so you should also honor your own thinking by presenting it clearly and supporting it with research.

1.4.2 Sources need something to support.

To accept that your ideas are the star in a research paper is to throw down a gauntlet of challenge to yourself: You must produce the star—the ideas. That is, as you research and write, you must supply not only the central idea you wish to advance, but also the analysis, synthesis, fresh insights, interpretations, conclusions, reasons, examples, and other information that drive your central idea forward and that are supported by your research. When you bring in a source, it should have a clear role in adding weight and credibility to your line of thinking or argument.

Henry Ford is credited with having said, "Thinking is the hardest work there is, which is why so few people do it." If he is correct, that may explain why so many research papers handed in to instructors contain little more than a series of thoughtlessly pasted-together quotations. Do not let your papers descend to this level. If you do, you will lose most of the benefits of writing a research paper while reducing your workload only slightly.

1.4.3 Sources need interpreting.

Think of your role as the writer of a research paper, not as an antiquarian collector of old quotations fit to be put on display, but as a detective, a solver of a puzzle, making sense out of many different elements of information. So much information, so many viewpoints, all this raw data in need of explanation—all the materials you locate in your research need more than just organizing, but they also require sorting out and applying to a central conclusion. Much thinking and much writing must come in connection with the use of your sources as you explain the meaning, implications, and effect of each one. Forget the staplers (those who would merely staple together an assortment of source materials); you are the weaver of a beautiful and sensible tapestry. You must ultimately tell the story that the sources have helped you to discover.

Review questions.

To see how well you understand this chapter, attempt to answer each of the following questions without referring to the text. (Write down your answers to make checking easier.) Then check your answers with the text. If you missed something important, add it to your answer.

1. What are the benefits sources provide to a researcher?

2. Explain how the use of sources strengthens your writing.

3. Discuss the reasons for citing sources.

4. What is meant by the statement, "Your thinking is the star"?

Questions for thought and discussion.

Use these questions for in-class discussion or for stimulating your own thinking.

1. Think about the last paper you wrote. Apart from the new knowledge you gained about the subject, did you learn anything else, such as thinking skills or writing skills?

2. Have you ever written a research paper where you commented very little on your sources? If so, do you think you learned less than if you had written more about the sources?

3. Has this chapter made you more enthusiastic about writing a research paper? Why or why not?

4. Has this chapter convinced you of the value of citation? Why or why not?

Name _____   Course _____

Chapter 1 Review: True-false quiz.

Directions: Based on your knowledge of Chapter 1, determine whether each statement below is true or false.

1. Citations are merely for academic accountability and do not help the reader of the paper.
   ☐ True   ☐ False

2. The sources used in a research paper should support the writer's ideas.
   ☐ True   ☐ False

3. Citing sources weakens the writer's own argument.
   ☐ True   ☐ False

4. A writer's own ideas are stimulated by reading others' ideas.
   ☐ True   ☐ False

5. Citing the sources used in a paper is important for avoiding plagiarism.
   ☐ True   ☐ False

6. Mentioning opposing sources in a paper on a controversial topic weakens the paper.
   ☐ True   ☐ False

7. Knowing how to write well is an academic skill that usually will have little application after graduation.
   ☐ True   ☐ False

8. Writing helps people discover what they think about something.
   ☐ True   ☐ False

9. Because a research paper relies heavily on sources, it will therefore have little or nothing original in it.
   ☐ True   ☐ False

10. Because most of your sources are written by highly educated writers, you will not need to explain what a quotation means.
    ☐ True   ☐ False

Self-Assessments.

On the following pages are several self-assessments you can take to determine your attitudes and knowledge about plagiarism and citation requirements. After you have read this book and worked through the exercises, you can take these assessments again to measure what you have learned. A preliminary assessment is valuable for learning about what you already know and what you still need to know. It also focuses your attention on the concepts of importance, so that as you read the book you will be on the alert. A postassessment is valuable for discovering what you have learned. You can compare your pre- and postscores to learn how your attitudes and knowledge have changed.

Name _____   Course _____

Self-Assessment: Researched writing survey.

Directions: This survey is designed to discover how confident you now feel about several skills and tasks related to the writing process. There are no right or wrong answers. Please respond to each question by putting a mark at a point along the scale that best represents your opinion.

1. When you are assigned a research paper in a course, do you welcome it as an opportunity to learn, or do you see it as a burden or unwelcome task?

    Welcome   Neutral   Unwelcome
    □ ---------- □ ----------□ ---------- □ ---------- □ ---------- □ ---------- □

2. How confident are you in your ability to use supporting material (quotations, examples, research) effectively to strengthen your ideas in a paper?

    Very Confident   Neutral   Not At All Confident
    □ ---------- □ ----------□ ---------- □ ---------- □ ---------- □ ---------- □

3. How confident are you in your ability to paraphrase an idea for use in a research paper?

    Very Confident   Neutral   Not At All Confident
    □ ---------- □ ----------□ ---------- □ ---------- □ ---------- □ ---------- □

4. How much formal training have you had regarding plagiarism and how to avoid it?

    Very Much   Some   None
    □ ---------- □ ----------□ ---------- □ ---------- □ ---------- □ ---------- □

5. In writing a research paper, how easy have you found it to incorporate sources that conflict with your central argument or idea?

    Very Easy   Somewhat Challenging   Very Difficult
    □ ---------- □ ----------□ ---------- □ ---------- □ ---------- □ ---------- □

6. How confident are you that you know the rules for using sources well enough to avoid unintentional plagiarism?

    Very Confident   Neutral   Not At All Confident
    □ ---------- □ ----------□ ---------- □ ---------- □ ---------- □ ---------- □

Name _____   Course _____

Self-Assessment: Rules of citation quiz.

Directions: Based on your knowledge, decide whether each statement is true or false.

1. When you use an idea you found in a source, you do **not** need to cite the idea if you put it entirely into your own words.
   ☐ True   ☐ False

2. As long as you put the author's name at the end of the paragraph, you may use the author's exact words, without needing quotation marks or a block indentation.
   ☐ True   ☐ False

3. In a research paper, you must cite every fact and idea that is not your own, such as the date Pearl Harbor was attacked by the Japanese.
   ☐ True   ☐ False

4. If you copy a paragraph from an old work that is no longer copyrighted, you still must show it is quoted and cite it, even though it is now in the public domain.
   ☐ True   ☐ False

5. Anything posted on the Web is common knowledge and therefore can be used without citation.
   ☐ True   ☐ False

6. Common knowledge does not need to be cited, unless you quote the exact words of the source (such as an encyclopedia).
   ☐ True   ☐ False

7. If a source presents your own opinion better than you could express it, then you can copy those words into your paper without quotation marks or citation.
   ☐ True   ☐ False

8. If you summarize the general argument of a book into a paragraph of your own words, you still must cite the source.
   ☐ True   ☐ False

9. Plagiarism refers only to copying a source's words without citation: You cannot plagiarize ideas.
   ☐ True   ☐ False

10. There is no such thing as "unintentional plagiarism."
    ☐ True   ☐ False

11. If you copy a drawing or map and use it in your paper, you must cite the source because those are also forms of ideas.
    ☐ True   ☐ False

Name _____   Course _____

Self-Assessment: Plagiarism attitude scale.

Directions: This is a measure of your opinions and attitudes about plagiarism. It is not a test. There are no right or wrong answers. Please indicate your honest opinion about each item.

1. I might accidentally commit plagiarism because I'm **not** sure what it is.
   ☐ Strongly Agree   ☐ Agree   ☐ Neutral   ☐ Disagree   ☐ Strongly Disagree

2. Cheating on a test is a worse offense than copying a few paragraphs from a source into one's paper without citing them.
   ☐ Strongly Agree   ☐ Agree   ☐ Neutral   ☐ Disagree   ☐ Strongly Disagree

3. I would never knowingly commit plagiarism.
   ☐ Strongly Agree   ☐ Agree   ☐ Neutral   ☐ Disagree   ☐ Strongly Disagree

4. Plagiarism is important only to people trying to protect their copyright profits.
   ☐ Strongly Agree   ☐ Agree   ☐ Neutral   ☐ Disagree   ☐ Strongly Disagree

5. If plagiarism is widespread at a school, a student would be justified in plagiarizing in order to keep up with the competition.
   ☐ Strongly Agree   ☐ Agree   ☐ Neutral   ☐ Disagree   ☐ Strongly Disagree

6. If my roommate gives me permission to use his or her paper for one of my classes, I don't think there is anything wrong with doing that.
   ☐ Strongly Agree   ☐ Agree   ☐ Neutral   ☐ Disagree   ☐ Strongly Disagree

7. Plagiarism is against my ethical values.
   ☐ Strongly Agree   ☐ Agree   ☐ Neutral   ☐ Disagree   ☐ Strongly Disagree

8. It's okay to use something you have written in the past to fulfill a new assignment because you can't plagiarize yourself.
   ☐ Strongly Agree   ☐ Agree   ☐ Neutral   ☐ Disagree   ☐ Strongly Disagree

9. If I lend a paper to another student to look at, and then that student turns it in as his or her own and is caught, I should **not** be punished also.
   ☐ Strongly Agree   ☐ Agree   ☐ Neutral   ☐ Disagree   ☐ Strongly Disagree

10. Even if they never get caught, plagiarizers cheat themselves.
    ☐ Strongly Agree   ☐ Agree   ☐ Neutral   ☐ Disagree   ☐ Strongly Disagree

11. Students caught plagiarizing should be punished as harshly as other cheaters.
    ☐ Strongly Agree   ☐ Agree   ☐ Neutral   ☐ Disagree   ☐ Strongly Disagree

2
Avoiding Plagiarism

It is the little writer rather than the great writer who never seems to quote, and the reason is that he is never really doing anything else.
—Havelock Ellis

An important part of using sources effectively lies in distinguishing between your own ideas and the ideas that come from outside sources. This chapter presents the rules about what and when to cite and teaches you how to avoid plagiarism.

♦ Learning about the various forms of plagiarism (intentional and unintentional) will enable you to avoid them.

♦ Committing intentional plagiarism harms the plagiarizer.

♦ Knowing what to cite makes citation easier.

♦ Learning about the myths surrounding citation will keep you from being deceived.

♦ Taking steps to protect yourself against a false charge of plagiarism is an important practice.

2.1 What is plagiarism?

In essence, plagiarism is a simple concept: When you make use of words, ideas, or any information from a source other than your own knowledge and experience, you must give credit to the source in a citation. Not giving credit to such borrowed intellectual material is plagiarism. There are a few complicating factors (such as *common knowledge*, discussed later on), but what appears to confuse the most people over this issue are uncertainties about the details and exceptions. Circulating on many campuses is a significant amount of wrong information about what needs to be cited and what constitutes appropriate citation.

2.1.1 A working definition of plagiarism.

Perhaps the best way to clarify what plagiarism is (and is not) is to begin with a simple definition and then explain its meaning. Therefore, we will begin with this definition:

Plagiarism occurs when an information source is not properly credited.

As you read and contemplate this brief definition, think about some of the implications. Specifically, note the following.

♦ **Plagiarism is often unintentional.** Thus, it is not defined only as the *intentional* failure to credit an information source.

♦ **A source may be credited, but *improperly* credited.** Thus, there may still be plagiarism even though a citation is present.

♦ **Copyright is irrelevant.** The definition does not mention the legal status (copyright, public domain, permission to use, etc.) of the information because those elements are not relevant to the plagiarism issue.

♦ **The location and format of the source are irrelevant.** The source of the information (such as the Internet) has no bearing on the need to cite. See Section 2.3.1 below.

2.1.2 Intentional plagiarism.

This is the kind of plagiarism most people think of when the subject is brought up: deliberate cheating on an assignment by copying a few sentences, a few paragraphs, or even an entire paper without quoting or citing the source. It is no secret to students—or to their instructors—that entire research papers are available both free and for sale on the Web, that journal articles can be copied from electronic databases, and that some students share their papers with each other. And, of course, every instructor knows how some students copy sentences and paragraphs from hither and yon and paste them into their papers without attribution.

This behavior, which amounts to stealing someone else's words and ideas and lying to the instructor by claiming them as the student's own, is highly offensive. Such complete disrespect for the academic enterprise (contempt for fellow students as well as instructors) is therefore punished harshly in most cases. A failing grade on the assignment is usually the most gentle penalty, with failure in the course more common. In higher education, expulsion from the college or university is not at all uncommon. That said, there are better reasons to avoid intentional plagiarism than merely fear of punishment. See Section 2.2 below on ethics.

Actions That Constitute Plagiarism

Downloading and turning in a paper from the Web, including a Web page or a paper mill essay	Including a graph, table, or picture from a source without proper citation
Copying and pasting phrases, sentences, or paragraphs into your paper without showing a quotation and adding proper citation	Getting so much help from a tutor or writing helper that the paper or part of the paper is no longer honestly your own work
Paraphrasing or summarizing a source's words or ideas without proper citation	Turning in previously written work when that practice is prohibited by your instructor

---

2.1.3 Unintentional plagiarism.

Recall that our definition states, "Plagiarism occurs when an information source is not properly credited." The definition does not say whether or not the writer *intended* to provide proper credit. Thus, it is possible to commit plagiarism without intent. The causes of unintentional plagiarism are several, such as lack of knowledge of proper source use, misunderstanding the rules for citation, careless note taking, reliance on uninformed opinion about citing, and carelessness in the application of the rules of citation.

Sometimes, a significant source of unintentional plagiarism is the overuse or improper use of a tutor or editor. Be careful not to cross the line between getting advice and having a tutor contribute to your paper without acknowledgment. Writing tutors should not write sentences for you or make major changes to your own work. You may want to check institutional policy here, especially if you have a friend help you with your papers.

Chapters 4 and 5 of this book are dedicated to guiding you through the proper and effective use of source material so that you can avoid other forms of unintentional plagiarism.

2.1.4 Self-recycling.

Self-recycling involves a student's use of his or her own writing. Common examples include using a paper from a previous course in another course, turning in the same paper to two different instructors during the same term, or using portions of previously written work in new work. In surveys taken at the university level, most students believed that self-recycling was permissible, thinking, "You can't plagiarize yourself." However, many professors and their institutions disagree. The purpose of a writing assignment is not simply to create work that you can reduce by recycling previous work. Rather, the writing assignment provides you with an opportunity to explore a subject, hone your research skills, improve your thinking and analyzing abilities, and practice your writing skills. Remember this:

The goal of education is not to get through, but to get better.

Copying and pasting your own previous work short-circuits this intention just as effectively as copying and pasting text from somewhere else. For this reason, self-recycling and multiple submission of papers are usually prohibited. If you have questions about self-recycling or multiple submission of papers, consult your instructor or ask about institutional policy.

2.2 Why you should avoid intentional plagiarism.

Many of the materials in this book will help you avoid unintentional plagiarism by training you in the proper use of sources: when to cite, how to cite, and how to build sources into your writing, both correctly and effectively. Avoiding intentional plagiarism, on the other hand, must be a matter of personal choice on your part. If you are wondering why you should not cheat, consider the following points:

2.2.1 Intentional plagiarism harms your character.

Would you like to have a friend who is a thief and a liar, acts pridefully superior to others, and takes advantage of others' honesty? Those who turn in the work of another as their own are doing exactly that. First, they steal another's words or ideas; then they lie about it by claiming authorship for them. Next, they turn in the paper, knowing that the instructor will expend pointless time and effort grading a paper and making comments that will have no effect on the students' learning. Last, they secretly sneer at those students who have made the effort to write their own paper, and, if the course is based on a curve, may actually harm the honest students' grades.

The fact is, our character is shaped by what we do. The person who cheats on research papers is rapidly losing personal integrity, and that loss will be reflected in other areas of life as well. For this reason, one of the most important results of formal education is who you become. Knowledge is important, and developing skills (such as thinking and writing) is important. But becoming a person of integrity—someone who can be trusted, someone who tells the truth—is indeed crucial. The habits you develop in college are likely to stay with you throughout your working life.

2.2.2 Follow the Golden Rule.

Many writers, religious leaders, and philosophers have advocated the Golden Rule, "Behave toward others the same way you want them to behave toward you," because this rule helps hold the fabric of society together. If you cheat and others cheat, how will anyone ever be able to trust anyone else? Would you want to have heart surgery by a doctor who cheated through medical school? Would you want an attorney who cheated through law school? Would you even want an auto mechanic who cheated on the licensing exams? If you think it is all right for you to cheat, why should others do differently?

2.2.3 Intentional plagiarizers cheat themselves.

Chapter 1, Section 1.1, discussed the importance of learning how to write and think because most people will need these skills in whatever career they choose. Turning in a copied paper or even a paper assembled from copied parts prevents the development of these writing and thinking skills as well as the skills of researching, organizing, planning, and attention to detail—all of which are highly valued by those who hire and promote employees. Thus, by not learning how to work with information in an economy based on working with information, intentional plagiarizers are cheating themselves out of future success. They also cheat themselves out of part of their education by not gaining the knowledge and insights that researching and writing a paper would have given them.

2.3 Guidelines for citation.

The definition of plagiarism on the first page of this chapter tells us that an *information source* must be cited. An information source refers to any producer of information other than your own observation, knowledge, or experience. This idea can be expressed in another way as a working rule for citation:

If the information came from outside your own head, cite the source.

The term *information* here will be interpreted quite broadly. The following sections will clarify the rule.

2.3.1 What needs to be cited?

The rather broad word *information* is used in the definitions above because breadth is needed to include all the forms of borrowed intellectual material (to use an even broader term) now available to you. The early definitions of plagiarism and the rules for citation used terms such as *borrowed words or ideas,* but phrases like this are clearly too limiting. The table below shows many kinds of intellectual property or information products in need of citation when you make use of them in your research papers. The list is not intended to be exhaustive, but rather to allow you to see the breadth of possibility. The following sections provide further guidelines.

What to Cite

You must cite someone else's	You do not have to cite your own
words you quote	words
words you summarize	idea (interpretation, opinion, conclusion)
words you paraphrase	data
idea (interpretation, opinion, conclusion)	graph
data	photograph
graph	drawing
photograph	table of information
drawing	computer program code
table of information	experiment
computer program code	survey
experiment	example
survey	unique concept
example	apt phrase
unique concept	expression of common knowledge
apt phrase (e.g., "flat-tire thinking")	solution to a problem
expression of common knowledge	
solution to a problem	
speech or audio recording	
video source (film, TV program)	
the structure or sequencing of facts, ideas, or arguments (e.g., from an encyclopedia)	

Remember: The *location* of the information source (such as the Web, a speech, or a book) and the *format* of the information (printed, digital, audio, video, live person) are irrelevant. You must cite all of the sources of information that you use, regardless of location or format.

2.3.2 What about common knowledge?

There is one exception to the rule of citing all outside information. Common knowledge does not need to be cited. Common knowledge includes whatever an educated person would be expected to know or could locate in an ordinary encyclopedia. It represents the kind of general information found in many sources and remembered by many people. Here are some of the types of common knowledge:

♦ **Easily observable information.** For example, heat makes people tired in summer; puppies display tremendous energy; most teenagers like chocolate; mud can be very sticky; certain types of trees lose their leaves in the fall; the First Amendment to the U. S. Constitution concerns freedom of speech and religion; the freeways are crowded at rush hour in many large cities.

♦ **Commonly reported facts.** For example, poet George Herbert was born in 1593 and died in 1633; Napoleon's army was decimated by the winter march on Moscow during the War of 1812; the Concorde passenger jet was developed jointly by the British and French; automobile tires are made from rubber compounds; cigarette smoking can cause health problems.

♦ **Common sayings.** For example, traditional proverbs need no citation: "Waste not, want not"; "Look before you leap"; "He who hesitates is lost." Some quotations have become proverbial as well, such as Alexander Pope's "Fools rush in where angels fear to tread." (Quoting more than this commonly spoken line would require a citation.)

There are some cautions to the above:

♦ **Finding the same information in several places does not automatically make it common knowledge.** Especially on the Web, information gets posted and reposted on many sites. A dozen sites selling the same vitamins or advancing the same political ideas may all have the same information, but that does not make the information common knowledge (or even reliable). Commonly expressed claims (that may be controversial) are not the same as common knowledge. Common knowledge means just that: generally accepted information of a factual or historical nature.

♦ **Quoting a source presenting common knowledge requires citation.** While common knowledge by itself need not be cited, *the source of the specific expression of common knowledge must be identified.* For example, you may mention without citation, as above, that Napoleon's army suffered ruinous losses during the march on Moscow. However, if your source says, "Napoleon's army froze in droves as it struggled ever so futilely toward Moscow," you must use quotation marks and cite the source of those words, if you use them. Therefore, if you use someone's words, you must quote and cite them, even if they contain an idea that is common knowledge.

♦ **An organized body of common knowledge needs citation.** A fact or two of common knowledge taken from an encyclopedia need not be cited. However, you may not summarize or paraphrase long passages without citation because the structure of information (its sequencing, emphasis, and selection) is not common knowledge and will need attribution.

♦ **Common knowledge is often intermingled with interpretation.** In many sources, common knowledge facts are mixed with analysis, interpretation, and opinion. All such commentary on common knowledge must be cited. For example, if your source says that operating the space shuttle program is an expensive project, that would not need citation, since it is common knowledge. However, if your source uses the word *wasteful* instead of (or in addition to) *expensive*, that is interpretation and would need citation.

♦ **You may not always know what is common knowledge.** When you encounter a fact that you believe might be common knowledge, but you are unsure, follow the rule of uncertainty:

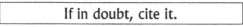

> **If in doubt, cite it.**

It is much better to cite unnecessarily than to neglect citing something that should have been cited. If you have a large amount of common knowledge, such as some biographical details of a famous writer, it may be easier to paraphrase or summarize a single source (and cite it) than to assemble the many pieces from various general references.

♦ **Sometimes common knowledge sources disagree.** General sources may differ about the dates of certain events, the number of people involved, or even the definition of a term. If you are aware of such disagreement, you should cite the source you use or use and cite both (or all) pieces of conflicting information.

♦ **Common knowledge is not always true.** Sometimes, what "everybody knows" is not even correct. For example, the common belief that people should drink eight glasses of water a day is more myth than fact. The claim looks like a piece of common knowledge because it is repeated everywhere, yet there appears to be no scientific basis for it. Unless you are quite certain about a claim being both common and correct, you might want to cite the source or perform further research to resolve the issue.

This section can be summed up by the following decision tree, which helps you decide when to cite by asking just two questions:

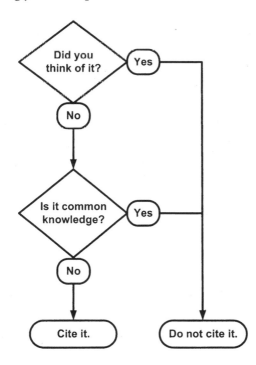

When Should You Cite?

2.3.3 Will my paper be nothing but citations?

A common fear or objection to the rule that all borrowed information must be cited is that such a practice will make the student's paper nothing but citations. However, as we noted in Chapter 1, sources and their citations support your own thinking and analysis. Your assignment is to *write* a research paper, not to *glue together* a research paper by using a few transitional expressions to connect a handful of sources. Much of the paper should consist of your own thinking, analysis, interpretation, examples, commentary, fresh ideas, judgments, explanations, anecdotes, evaluation of data, and so on.

2.3.4 Do you ever have to cite yourself?

The surprising answer is, Yes. If you have created a previous work, such as an experiment you performed and wrote up, a short film, survey analysis, formal speech, and so on, you must cite it if you quote or refer to it in a new work. If you perform the experiment for the paper you are working on, then you do not cite it. Whatever you have written or created before becomes a potential source that you then should cite when you borrow from it. Yes, you can even quote yourself (though, of course, discretion is advised). An exception to this rule would be a case where an instructor allows you to make use of previous work to generate new work, as in taking an old paper and revising it into a new paper, or using sections of previous work in a new work.

2.4 Myths and facts about citing.

This section is intended to clear up many of the misconceptions about the use of various kinds of information available to you, by exposing and correcting some of the myths about citing. A myth in the sense used here means a wrong belief, often spread around commonly by others who do not know the facts.

2.4.1 The public domain myth.

Myth: You can quote anything that is in the public domain or no longer copyrighted without having to cite the source.

Fact: As mentioned above, the legal status of a piece of information has no bearing on whether or not it needs to be cited. Words, ideas, or other kinds of information taken from a source must be cited, whether the information is copyrighted or in the public domain. Do not confuse information that is in the public domain with information that is common knowledge. Public domain information is now owned by the public, so that no royalties need be paid for its reproduction. However, most of this information is not common knowledge, so the source of any borrowed words or ideas from this public domain material must still be cited.

2.4.2 The fair use myth.

Myth: Even if a work is copyrighted, I can use it without attribution because I have *fair use* under copyright law.

Fact: This myth arises from a confusion similar to that just above. Fair use allows you to quote a source without payment or written permission. (For example, you can quote a dozen lines from a copyrighted poem in order to analyze it in a paper you are writing for a class, without having to pay the copyright holder a royalty.) Fair use, however, does not permit you to steal the author's words by claiming them as your own. In fact, if you do plagiarize a copyrighted source, you may be guilty not only of plagiarism (an academic dishonesty offense) but also of copyright infringement (a civil, and in some cases criminal, offense). The information on the next page shows the relationship and differences between plagiarism and copyright infringement.

Plagiarism and Copyright Infringement

Plagiarism and copyright infringement both refer to violations of intellectual property standards, but the two violations are different. Plagiarism is an ethical violation relating to a lack of proper attribution for borrowed material. Copyright infringement is a legal violation relating to the misuse of intellectual property, usually for financial gain. The differences can be clarified by the following example. Imagine that I start a publishing company called Bob's Press and I publish the four books below.

The first book, *Gulliver's Travels* by Jonathan Swift, is in the public domain because it was first published in 1726 and all copyrights have long since expired. So I can publish this book or parts of it without copyright infringement. Further, as long as I accurately attribute the text I publish to its real author, I do not commit plagiarism. The second book, however, commits plagiarism because now I am claiming to be the author of a work that I did not write. I am still not guilty of copyright infringement, though, since the book is not copyrighted. The third book, *The Hunt for Red October* by Tom Clancy, accurately lists its real author, so I am not guilty of plagiarism by reprinting it. However, Mr. Clancy's publisher would be highly upset if I did so, because that would be copyright infringement. The book is still copyrighted and I do not have the rights to print the book. The fourth book would commit both plagiarism and copyright infringement because it claims that I am the author of a work I did not write (plagiarism) and it unlawfully uses copyrighted intellectual property.

2.4.3 The World Wide Web myth.

Myth: Whatever is on the Web is common knowledge, so it is permissible to use anything there without quotation marks or attribution.

Fact: This myth contains two errors. First, much of the information on the Web is not common knowledge. The Web is filled with unique facts, interpretations, opinions, commentaries, creative works, original articles, and much more. The second error is that even what is common knowledge on the Web or elsewhere cannot be quoted word-for-word without citation. The quotation of any words from a source needs to have quotation marks (or a block quotation) and a citation. (Note in the table under Section 2.3.1 that the "expression of common knowledge" is listed under what needs to be cited.)

It should also be noted in relation to this myth that most of what is on the Web is also copyrighted. Web pages, letters, e-mail, and other forms of written communication are now automatically copyrighted as soon as they are written down. It is no longer necessary to register writing with the copyright office in order to be protected. And note that copyright also applies to photographs, drawings, and other intellectual property on the Web.

2.4.4 The encyclopedia myth.

Myth: Because encyclopedias contain common or general knowledge, I can copy from them without having to cite them.

Fact: While it is true that common knowledge (such as the dates of birth and death of Abraham Lincoln, or the names of the fifty states) does not need attribution, quoting an encyclopedia (which may not be a very scholarly practice anyway) does require attribution and quotation marks for two reasons. First, *whenever* you copy words, you must use quotation marks or a block indentation (and a citation in each case) to show that you are quoting. Second, there is much more in encyclopedias than common knowledge facts. Attribution is required for any source (including encyclopedias) from which you get judgments, conclusions, viewpoints, interpretations, thoughts, ideas, evaluations, specific words or phrases, findings, controversial facts, or even interesting questions. As mentioned in Section 2.3.2, the best rule to follow here is, "If in doubt, cite it." Even if you think you have an item of common knowledge, reference its source. Overcitation is never a vice; undercitation is never a virtue.

2.4.5 The paraphrased paper myth.

Myth: If I change a common knowledge source into my own words, I can use the whole source without attribution.

Fact: As you will discover during the discussion of paraphrasing in Chapter 4, the structure and sequence of ideas are considered unique to the writer and are therefore not common knowledge. You can use a fact or two from a common knowledge source without citation, but to copy the same structure and order of facts, even in your own words, would be to commit plagiarism. If you think about it for a moment, you will see that if the wholesale paraphrasing of common knowledge were allowed, it would defeat the purpose of writing research papers because students would be merely replacing words rather than performing the tasks of researching, analyzing, and integrating sources into their own writing.

2.4.6 The friend's permission myth.

Myth: If my friend gives me permission to use his or her paper, I can turn it in as my own without being guilty of plagiarism, because I am not stealing my friend's words or ideas.

Fact: If you are writing an academic research paper, there is no circumstance where you are permitted to present the words of another as your own. (Even if you are writing a paper as a team, you are claiming that the team is the true author of the words of the paper, except where items have been clearly quoted.) No source can elect not to be cited. Another way to say this is that no one can give you permission to deceive your instructor into thinking you wrote something you did not write. Even sources that want to remain anonymous must be cited—as anonymous sources.

2.4.7 The named source myth.

Myth: If I mention the author's name in the text, I can copy word-for-word and quotation marks are not necessary.

Fact: All quotations require either quotation marks or block indentations. All text in your paper without one of these is assumed to have been written by you.

2.4.8 The converted words myth.

Myth: If I turn the source's words completely into my own words, then the words and ideas become my own, and I do not need to cite the source.

Fact: You cannot write a source out of existence by changing words around. Putting a source's words completely into your own words is an effective strategy known as paraphrasing. Yet every paraphrase must be cited because every source must be cited. The origin of *ideas* as well as words needs proper attribution.

2.4.9 The tiny theft myth.

Myth: If I use only a few words from a source, I don't need to cite them.

Fact: Every quoted word needs to be cited (as well as placed in quotation marks). The best example of quoting just a few words is the *apt phrase*, two or three words that provide a flair or flavor from a source. Sometimes the phrase is simply unusual or artistic, as in an alliteration such as "clandestine coup." Often, the apt phrase is a colorful metaphor, as in "pretzeled logic." Whatever the case, borrowed words must be quoted and cited.

2.4.10 The background information myth.

Myth: I just used the source for background information but did not actually cite any part of it, so all I needed to do was list the source in the bibliography.

Fact: If you use information from a source in your paper, you must cite where you use it. Any item of background information you mention must be cited unless it is common knowledge. Remember that a use includes paraphrase, summary, brief mention, or even an isolated fact, not just a quotation or direct reference to the author's interpretation. If the source contained only common knowledge that you therefore did not cite, do not list the source in the bibliography. The References list (APA) and Works Cited list (MLA) should contain only those works explicitly referred to in your paper.

The Golden Test

You can avoid worrying about all the myths above by relying instead on a simple test for deciding whether or not you need to cite a piece of information. The test involves asking yourself about how your reader might understand the source of the information. In other words, ask the question, "Will my reader likely believe that this information originated with me when it did not?" If the answer is "Yes," then you need a citation to correct your reader's misunderstanding.

2.5 Protecting against a false charge of plagiarism.

If you need proof of the value of someone's writing as intellectual property, take note of the fact that student research papers are now being stolen and sold or traded to others (both on campus and on the Web). Imagine your dismay if you, as an honest student, work hard to produce a great research paper, only to be confronted by your instructor, who says that your paper is available on the Web or has been flagged as containing plagiarism by a commercial plagiarism service. Following are some steps you can take to protect yourself from a problem like this.

2.5.1 Protect your data and passwords.

An individual research paper can require dozens of hours of work; the papers you have completed can therefore represent hundreds of hours of mental effort. If they are saved on a floppy disk or CD-R or flash memory stick, they are neatly packaged and handy for any thief. Even printouts require only a few minutes to scan and convert back into electronic format ready for editing and a false claim of authorship by a thief. To those who would like to skip the labor but get the credit for it, your work is a valuable commodity. Your stolen papers could be turned in by the thief, sold to another student, or uploaded to a paper mill site in trade for another paper. Therefore, whatever storage method you use—printout, floppy disk, Zip disk, CD-R, flash memory stick, your PC's hard drive, a network drive, a Web storage service, or some other medium—be certain that you keep your work secure from potential thieves.

2.5.2 Do not lend, give, or upload any paper.

Many professors wish they had a dollar for every time they have heard of a student who lent a paper to another student "to look at" or "for reference," only to have that other student turn the paper in, claiming to have written it. If your paper is turned in by someone else, you may be accused of being an accessory to plagiarism. At the very least, you should not want your work to be stolen in that way.

As mentioned in Section 2.5.1 above, another risk now is that if you lose possession of your paper, it may be uploaded to a mill site in trade for another paper or simply as a gift to others. Should your professor search the Web and locate your paper on a mill site, you may be accused of having downloaded it from the site.

Be wise, therefore, and remember that lending your disk, e-mailing your paper, giving out your password, letting a friend use your computer, or even lending a printout puts you at great risk. If you are persuaded to let a friend look at one of your papers, show it while you are present, if possible. Once the paper is out of your sight, you cannot know what might happen to it.

2.5.3 Report any theft immediately.

Should you know or believe that one or more of your papers might have been stolen or otherwise compromised, report that fact immediately. If a paper you are working on or have just handed in is stolen, inform the instructor in the class for which it is due. If the term has ended, you should still report the theft, either to the instructor, the department, a dean, or other person. Ask one of your instructors about institutional policy on this issue.

2.5.4 Save and print all drafts and notes.

Take a moment to imagine that you are an instructor grading research papers. You read one that is very good. Just to be cautious, you check for the paper on the Web, and to your surprise, you find it on a mill site. You call in the student who handed in the paper. "Did you really write this paper?" you ask. "Yes," says the student. "Okay," you say, "show me your rough drafts." "I threw them all away," the student replies. After this exchange, would you be more suspicious of the authorship or less?

Whatever your answer, you should be able to see that a good way to protect yourself from a false charge of plagiarism is to keep all the evidence that you really did write the paper: the note cards, printouts, drafts, scratch outlines, or whatever else you may have. *Print out the current draft of your paper each time you work on it* so that you will have a printed record of its various stages of creation.

Imagine once again that you are an instructor. In looking over your grades, you notice that you have no grade for Jane's paper. You see her in class. "Jane, why didn't you turn in a paper?" you ask. "I did turn one in," Jane says. "Well," you say, "I didn't get it or I lost it. Bring me another copy tomorrow." "I can't," Jane tells you, "because I lost my disk." "Don't you have a copy of the paper?" you ask. "No," she answers.

What would you do in a circumstance like this? If you do what many instructors do, Jane will have to write another paper. Once again, do not underestimate the value of your work. Protect all those hours of work by keeping multiple copies in safe places.

2.5.5 Photocopy or print out and save all sources.

In addition to the drafts and working notes, among the most convincing evidence that you have written a paper are photocopies of all the sources you used, nicely marked with ink or highlighter as you read through them and organized quotations or other references for use in your paper. If you can put photocopied pages and Web printouts on your instructor's desk and say, "Here are the sources of my quotations," you will most likely clear yourself in two minutes of any accusation that you downloaded the paper.

Because Web sites can change unpredictably, it is especially important to print out the material you use (or save the pages to disk). Journal articles from on-line databases should be printed out, while journal articles in print form can be photocopied. For books, photocopy only the title page and the pages you actually cite (whether you quote, paraphrase, summarize, or only refer to them).

More and more instructors are requiring these copies of sources to be made and submitted with the final version of the research paper. Even if copies are not required, however, they provide inexpensive insurance, as well as an excellent resource during the writing of your paper. See Chapter 3, Section 3.1.1, for more information.

2.5.6 Be proactive.

As you work on your paper, visit your instructor to ask for input and feedback. Input involves asking the instructor's advice about research strategies (such as where to look, what keywords to use, what sources are recommended, or what direction to pursue with your topic). Early on, feedback involves discussing the central idea you plan to support; later, it may include showing your instructor preliminary sections of the paper in order to ensure that you are fulfilling the requirements and are generally on the right track.

When you have a substantial draft, visit the writing center for help with structure or style (or even grammar and mechanics). Keep the marked-up draft. (Some writing centers have a stamp or require their tutors to sign drafts or pages of comments. If your center has such a policy, keep this evidence of your visit.) Feedback on drafts (from the instructor and the writing center) also provides you with the opportunity to be sure that you are incorporating sources properly and not inadvertently plagiarizing any of them. Be specific in your interest here, telling your instructor or tutor that you are concerned that all your sources receive proper acknowledgment.

To add unique content to your work, conduct your own survey to gather opinions about an aspect of your subject, or call or e-mail an expert for an interview. Perform an experiment or collect your own data by measuring or counting something relevant to your topic. (If you meet with your instructor for feedback as recommended above, ask about a useful experiment or survey you might perform.)

All of these steps will make your paper much better, and they will also establish a construction trail demonstrating that you have worked on the paper well in advance of the due date.

Review questions.

To see how well you understand this chapter, attempt to answer each of the following questions without referring to the text. (Write down your answers to make checking easier.) Then check your answers with the text. If you missed something important, add it to your answer.

1. In your own words, define *plagiarism.*

2. Describe the difference between intentional and unintentional plagiarism.

3. What is *self-recycling,* and why do most academic institutions prohibit it?

4. How do intentional plagiarizers hurt themselves?

5. Give examples of information *other than words* that must be cited.

6. Define *common knowledge* and give an example.

7. Explain the relationship between copyright and plagiarism.

8. What are some ways to protect yourself from a false charge of plagiarism?

Questions for thought and discussion.

Use these questions for in-class discussion or for stimulating your own thinking.

1. Have you ever been falsely accused of plagiarism? If so, how did you defend yourself?

2. Has this chapter convinced you that self-recycling is not in your own best interest? Why or why not?

3. Have you ever written a research paper in which you started with one idea but developed it into a very different idea because of the information you found in your sources?

4. Before reading this chapter, were you misled by any of the myths about citing? Do you now understand why they are incorrect?

Name _____   Course _____

Chapter 2 Review: True-false quiz.

Directions: In each case, determine whether the statement is true or false.

1. It is **not** possible to plagiarize something in the public domain.
   ☐ True   ☐ False

2. It is possible to commit plagiarism by accident.
   ☐ True   ☐ False

3. You cannot plagiarize yourself.
   ☐ True   ☐ False

4. You do **not** have to cite quoted common knowledge.
   ☐ True   ☐ False

5. Everything on the Web is in the public domain.
   ☐ True   ☐ False

6. Even if you turn a quotation entirely into your own words, you still have to cite the source.
   ☐ True   ☐ False

7. It is **not** plagiarism to turn in your friend's paper if you have your friend's permission to do so.
   ☐ True   ☐ False

8. If you copy and paste a photograph from a Web site into your paper, you must provide a citation for the photograph.
   ☐ True   ☐ False

9. You do **not** need to cite fewer that five quoted words.
   ☐ True   ☐ False

10. You can use a source, add a citation, and still be guilty of plagiarism.
   ☐ True   ☐ False

Name _____   Course _____

Chapter 2: Rules of citation quiz.

Directions: In each case, decide whether you must include a citation of the source for the information described.

1. In a book, you find the phrase "cultural tapeworm" and want to use it in your paper.
   ☐ Have to cite it   ☐ Do not have to cite it

2. You conduct a personal interview with a doctor to get information about treatment for skin rashes. You make your own notes. In your paper, you use information from the interview.
   ☐ Have to cite it   ☐ Do not have to cite it

3. You read in several different sources about how on-line day traders in the stock market have turned stock buying and selling into a form of recreational gambling. In your paper, you mention in your own words that for some people the stock market seems to have become another kind of gambling.
   ☐ Have to cite it   ☐ Do not have to cite it

4. You create and distribute a survey to shoppers at a mall, asking about the brands of clothing they prefer. You include a table of the results in your paper.
   ☐ Have to cite it   ☐ Do not have to cite it

5. In your paper, you write, "Neil Armstrong set foot on the moon." This is a fact you have read many times in the past and you now do not remember where.
   ☐ Have to cite it   ☐ Do not have to cite it

6. In a paperback almanac published last year, you locate a graph showing the historical rise of energy consumption in the United States. You include this graph in your paper.
   ☐ Have to cite it   ☐ Do not have to cite it

7. In your paper, you paraphrase but do not quote a federal government document that is not copyrighted.
   ☐ Have to cite it   ☐ Do not have to cite it

8. You decide to end your paper with a bit of ancient wisdom, so you quote the traditional old proverb, "Look before you leap."
   ☐ Have to cite it   ☐ Do not have to cite it

9. You are writing a paper on childbirth. On a Web page, you locate a photograph of a baby in its mother's arms and paste the photograph into your paper.
   ☐ Have to cite it   ☐ Do not have to cite it

10. You locate a brilliant argument in favor of an idea you are advancing in a paper. You decide to use this argument but turn it completely into your own words.
    ☐ Have to cite it   ☐ Do not have to cite it

Notes

3
Selecting Sources

There is no less invention in aptly applying a thought found in a book,
than in being the first author of the thought.
    —Pierre Bayle

Both the enormous quantity of information now av   .f quality make the task of choosing sources wisely more im   .apter offers some guidelines and ideas for helping to choose usefu   .ources.

♦ Collecting and organizing your sources carefully wiɩ   .ɔid repeated
research.

♦ Choosing appropriate types of sources will give you better mɑ.ɩerials to use in
your papers.

♦ Evaluating the quality and credibility of the sources is important.

♦ Using some sources that disagree or conflict can improve your paper—if you
handle the conflicts properly.

3.1 Collecting sources.

Potentially, the most frustrating part of writing a research paper is losing track of a
source. You may have a great quotation that brilliantly sums up your major point, only
to discover that you have lost the record of where you got it. Or you may have the
source, but note that you neglected to write down the entire bibliographical entry. These
oversights are all too common: Listen to the voice of experience and save yourself much
effort by following these guidelines:

3.1.1 Photocopy, print, or save your sources.

As you locate each useful source, make a personal copy of it. Articles from printed
journals can be photocopied; pages from chapters of books can also be photocopied; articles from the Web or electronic databases can be saved and printed out. The doctrine of
fair use under United States copyright law allows you to make a photocopy of a copyrighted article for personal use in scholarly work such as writing a research paper.

Why should you do this? There are several reasons:

♦ **A copy keeps the context.** A full copy of an article or section of a book allows
you to see the quotation or information in context. As you think through the information, the context may cause you to reevaluate your initial interpretation.

♦ **A copy is a handy source.** You can return to the source easily any time you wish.
You will not need to look it up again or revisit the library. As you write your paper, new ideas or altered directions may cause you to return to a source and use
something different or additional. The convenience of having the source always
at hand cannot be overstated.

♦ **A copy can be written on.** On a hard copy, you can write notes, highlight passages, fold down corners, or whatever else helps you process and use the source.

Reading an article on-line or in a printed journal and only making notes (whether handwritten or typed) is much less effective for most students than making copies and writing on them.

♦ **A copy is an easy reference.** You can double-check the accuracy of the quotations, the spelling of names or technical terms, and the correctness of numbers and other information before turning in the paper.

♦ **Copies may be required.** Many instructors require copies of sources to be turned in with the final draft of the research paper.

♦ **Copies can help establish authorship.** As mentioned in Chapter 2, source copies (especially marked-up source copies) provide evidence that will help defend you in the event you are falsely accused of plagiarism.

3.1.2 Get the full, exact bibliographic information the first time.

This advice seems to be obvious. However, experience shows that many times, especially with journal articles, students write down only the pages from which they quote and neglect to write down the beginning and ending pages (as in 126-142) required for the Works Cited or References page. The result is that these students must look up the source again, making another trip to the library or duplicating a search on a database.

If you follow the advice of Section 3.1.1 above, be sure that you photocopy the title page of any books you use. Because the copyright date is usually on the reverse side of the title page, write that date on the photocopied title page. Similarly, photocopy the cover or contents page of all journals, being sure you get the journal title, date, and volume information. When you photocopy an article, be sure that page numbers are clearly visible on each page. If not, write the correct ones on the pages before you leave the library.

For Web and electronic database sources, copy and paste the full URL (uniform resource locator—the Web address) from the location window to a file. When a Web page prints out, many of the URLs are too long to include on the printed page, so they are shortened, leaving you with only a partial address. Unless the URL is clearly short and prints out in its entirety on the page, be sure to copy it while you have the article on the screen.

Photographs, graphics, charts, tables, drawings, and other visual information taken from the Web present a special problem because when you save them to disk as individual graphic files, the URLs are not included. Take care, therefore, to note the URL of the graphic when you save it. A good practice is to print the page or article containing the graphic so that you have both the graphic in context and the URL of the source page. At the least, paste each graphic into a word processing file and include the URL of the source beneath the graphic. You also may want to include some notes explaining the significance of the graphic and how you plan to use it in your paper.

3.1.3 Organize your source materials.

If you make printouts and photocopies of your sources (even the ones you save to disk from electronic databases), you can keep them organized by putting them in a binder. Data files can be organized on a disk or other storage medium. As you read through your sources and begin to see where they might be used in your paper, you might use divider tabs to collect the sources in relevant sections. In addition to a printout of your electronic sources, you will benefit by saving them in data files. If you copy and paste your quotations from a file version of an article, the quotation will be exact and there will be none of the copying errors that can occur with hand copying. Be sure to include an accurate reference to the source for each copy-and-pasted quotation.

3.2 Selecting the kinds of sources you need.

The saying, "All sources look alike on a computer screen," cautions us to be careful to consider the wide range of materials available—both in kind and in quality—and to select those that best suit the task at hand. Resist the temptation to use just any sources that you locate; take some time to think about the kinds of information you need and how well the sources you locate meet those needs.

3.2.1 Choose the kind of information you need.

For building a solid research paper, you will need facts, of course, but you will also want expert interpretation of some of those facts, together with professional judgments about the importance of the information you are discussing. You may want reasoned arguments, creative ideas, personal examples, accounts of events, experiments, philosophical commentary, and so forth. Many sources contain more than one of these kinds of information, while others focus largely on one or two. If you keep in mind what kind of information you are seeking, you will be able to select sources more quickly and more effectively from among the items you locate.

3.2.2 Choose appropriate primary and secondary sources.

A primary source is an original source of information. Examples of primary sources include a historical document, an account of a laboratory experiment, a literary work, an eyewitness account, the original proposal of a new idea, or other original work. A secondary source offers interpretation of, or commentary on, a primary source. Examples of secondary sources would include encyclopedia articles that rely on a number of primary sources to construct a historical narrative, a work of literary criticism, an explanation of the political implications of a survey, and works that popularize newly reported discoveries or newly presented ideas.

Depending on the subject, the class level, the instructor, and a number of other factors, you may be using more of one kind of source than the other. Many instructors view the research paper as the construction of a secondary source, analyzing and commenting on a set of primary sources. In a literature course, you may use secondary sources to support your interpretation of a literary work (the primary source) as you create a secondary source of your own. In a history course, you may use both primary sources (laws, letters, diaries, works written during the period under study) and secondary sources (interpretive works by modern historians) to construct a paper. In the social and behavioral sciences, you may use primary sources (reports of empirical or original studies) and create some primary source material yourself by conducting your own experiment, observation, or interview.

When you have a choice, the use of primary sources is usually superior because you are dealing directly with the original work or evidence rather than seeing it through the lens of another interpreter. For this reason, relying on general encyclopedias for sources is often frowned upon because the articles in them are secondary sources or are themselves based on secondary sources. (Using an encyclopedia to give yourself an overview, background information, ideas for the direction you want to take, the general consensus of current thought, and so on is an excellent idea. However, your research should then take you far beyond that.)

3.2.3 Choose sources of appropriate scholarship.

Whether printed or online, publications exist along a range or at various levels of scholarliness. The concept of scholarliness refers to the level of expertise and learning brought to bear on a subject as well as the intended audience and even the nature of the information itself. Generally speaking, the more scholarly a work, the more care is taken with accuracy and completeness. The following chart will give an idea of the range of informational materials.

Variety of Scholarliness in Sources

Professional	Substantive	Popular	Sensational
Written by academics, scientists, or experts	Written by staff writer or expert	Written by staff writer or freelance journalist	Written by staff writer or freelance writer
Audience is other academics or those trained in the field	Audience is the well-educated public	Audience is general reader	Audience is less well educated
Purpose is to share findings or present theories: to inform	Purpose is to inform and to entertain	Purpose is to entertain and inform	Purpose is to entertain
Discussion often highly specific and sophisticated	Discussion more general, easier to understand	Discussion general and simplified	Discussion sensational and simplistic
Bibliography of sources always included	Some sources cited	Sources often not cited	Sources not cited
Article has been peer-reviewed or refereed by other scholars in the field	Article approved by editorial board	Article approved by editorial board or editor	Article approved by editor

You should not take this chart too literally: There are not exactly four kinds of publications, and there are exceptions to most of the comments made here. However, the chart can serve as a general model to give you a good sense of how the source, purpose, and quality of information varies. For much of your research, it is a good idea to restrict yourself to sources of a professional or substantive variety. Sometimes popular magazines offer useful material; but as entertainment values take on more importance than informational values, the degree of reliability of a source can sometimes suffer.

3.2.4 Avoid choosing a source simply because you agree with it.

If the sources you use are to add strength to your writing, they must be robustly credible, well reasoned, and fair. You may find sources that support the direction of your argument but that are unworthy of use because they lack the qualities that will gain your reader's confidence. When you refer to a source, you are saying something about the source (that it is worth listening to) and about yourself (that your judgment has approved its use in a formal presentation). In other words, a little of each source you use rubs off on you and your authorial reputation. If you use good sources, your reader will think better of you, seeing you as smart, educated, and discerning.

Ask a Librarian

An excellent way to get help in locating and selecting good sources is to talk to a reference librarian. Librarians have expertise in searching for and evaluating information, and they are also familiar with the library's collection of materials, the subject guides, online databases, and more.

3.2.5 Avoid quoting standard dictionaries.

Would you like to know the easiest way to make almost any instructor or educated reader cringe? Simply begin your paper with, "According to Webster's dictionary, the word _____ means...." Why is this? Consider the reasons for not quoting a dictionary:

- **Readers have their own dictionaries.** It is assumed that readers have a desk dictionary handy, and that if all that is wanted is a standard dictionary definition, they can look up the word themselves.
- **Most dictionary definitions are unhelpful.** Many definitions are, in fact, circular. "Wonderful: exciting wonder"; "Heartbreaker: a person causing heartbreak"; "Heater: an apparatus for heating." Even definitions that are not circular like these are often so condensed, generalized, or vague that they do not come near the meaning of the word as you are planning to develop it.
- **Dictionary definitions are descriptive and not prescriptive.** This means that if enough people use a word in a certain way, the dictionary will eventually list it, even though the word has not meant that in the past. For example, some dictionaries now list *imply* as one of the acceptable meanings of *infer*, and some list *continual* and *continuous* as having the same meaning.
- **You can write a better definition.** If you need the definition of an ordinary word, your own definition will be better. For everyday terms, such as *love*, *justice*, or *philanthropy*, a little thought and effort will produce a much better definition than that found in a typical desk dictionary.
- **Scholarly definitions are superior.** If you need a more specialized definition, consult a specialty dictionary, such as *The International Dictionary of Psychology*

(1995). There are specialized works like this in many fields. You might also quote the definition of a key term from a scholarly article. Scholarly definitions are often extensive and focused, and therefore quite helpful.

♦ **Quoting a dictionary is a red flag.** Quoting a definition at the beginning of a paper implies to an educated reader that the writer does not know how to start a paper (or continue a thought) and is falling back on what amounts to a cliché, and a thoughtless one at that. A paper (or speech, for that matter) beginning with "According to Webster's dictionary" tells the reader (or hearer) that the writer did not put much thought or research into the product and that there is little to be hoped for in the rest of the performance.

From these reasons, you can see that quoting a dictionary will actually weaken your writing, not strengthen it.

3.3 Using and abusing Internet sources.

The Internet is an amazing grab bag of information, ranging in quality and credibility from excellent to terrible. When you sit down to search the Web, the first thing to remember is that not all information is created equal. Your goal is not merely to find some pages that include your search terms, but to find accurate and reliable information from reputable sources. Cut-and-run searching, where a student grabs whatever comes up on the first page of results, usually produces poor quality papers. It also teaches students little about the research process.

3.3.1 Search for reliable sites.

As you will see in Section 3.4 below, one of the indicators of the quality of information is its source. We tend to believe those who have knowledge and experience in a subject over those who are expressing the opinion of the day. It is reasonable, then, that organizations specializing in a subject are likely to have better information than a Web page posted by an individual. To begin your topic search, rather than typing in a search phrase and seeing what pages come up, start by looking for sites (that is, organizations) related to your topic. A profitable way to do this is to use your favorite search tool, such as Google or Alltheweb, to type in your topic followed by one of these words: *institute, association, forum, foundation, institution.* For example, if you will be writing about peace and conflict in the Middle East, typing in *middle east institute* will return a number of organizations dealing with the Middle East. Try your search topic with each of the other words to locate more organizations.

Another way to locate information from organizations is to use the advanced search commands in the search tool to limit the search results to items in the .org and .gov domains. (The .org domain is for organizations, mostly nonprofit; the .gov domain is for government agencies.)

3.3.2 Look deeply into the results.

It is true that the major search engines are constantly tweaking their secret methods of ranking pages so that the best pages appear earliest in the results. However, unlike directories, search engines use computer-based formulas to do the ranking, so many times the pages that you want will be well after the first 10 or 20 displayed by the search tool. Good advice is to (1) craft your search phrase carefully, (2) use more than one phrase, and (3) take the time to look at the first 100 to 200 hits for each query. You can set some of the search engines to return 50 or 100 hits on each page, making scrolling through a large number much more efficient.

3.3.3 Understand the context of individual pages.

When you perform a general Web search, do not just grab a page that looks good and use it in your paper. Take some time to discover the context of the page. Try backing up your browser one directory at a time by cutting off each previous directory to see what larger site the page is part of. For example, if your located page has the URL of www.ag.auburn.edu/dept/entplp/bulletins/pinebarkbeetle/pinebarkbeetle.htm, trim off the words after the final virgule (the forward slash) and see what you get. In this example, trimming off pinebarkbeetle.htm results in a "forbidden" message, meaning that you cannot look at that directory. So trim off the words after the second to last slash. Then the third to last. In this example, you will now see the home page of the Entomology and Plant Pathology Department of Auburn University. That is the host for the information you located. It appears that this information has a degree of official support and is therefore likely to be of better quality than information that does not.

(Note: If you have the Google toolbar installed in your browser, you can click on the Web *Up* button to go back one directory with each click.)

It may be useful to look at the root Web site of the information also. In our example, the root site is the College of Agriculture at Auburn University. On the home page of the root site, you will often find an About link that will give you some information about the site, its purpose, its writers, and so forth. This may be helpful as you judge the site's quality.

Remember also that Web search engines also deliver non Web sources, such as newsgroup postings. Newsgroup postings range in quality from the word of experts to groundless rantings to intentional falsehoods designed for good or ill (stock price manipulation, for example) to plagiarized pieces of the writings of others. Be very careful to assess the quality of such sources before you make use of them.

3.3.4 Use the invisible Web.

A substantial amount of information posted on the Web is not indexed by the search engines. To get to this information, on the invisible or deep Web, you must go directly to the various sites that host the information. The extra effort needed to access this information is rewarded by the fact that this information is usually high in quality.

Many articles from magazines and journals are accessible through the databases on the invisible Web. For example, FindArticles.com and MagPortal.com both offer free, full-text articles from various print and online publications. Other sites, such as CompletePlanet.com and Profusion.com, allow access to many databases not indexed by general search engines such as Google.

3.3.5 Follow the links.

Use quality information to find other quality information. When you locate a site or article that you find valuable and credible, visit the links from there to the other information. Not all links are recommendations, of course, but another page deemed worth linking to by a site you find valuable can provide a good possibility for finding more useful and reliable information related to your topic.

3.3.6 Go beyond the Internet.

Even though you may be tempted to get all your research information from a Web search, you should expand your efforts to include printed books, printed journals, and other sources (microfiche, interviews, and perhaps recordings or videos). While the Web does contain billions of pages of information, much of it valuable, it still represents a limited source. You will get a much better and more professional picture of your subject by including non-Web sources, especially books, in your research. You will also develop much better researching skills.

You can perform some beyond-the-Web searching from your computer. Ask a reference librarian which electronic databases are available to you. These databases, such as ProQuest, InfoTrac, Ebsco Host, and JSTOR feature full-text articles from printed journals. Many public libraries also have some of these databases available to patrons, often accessible from home.

3.4 Evaluating sources.

Implied in Section 3.2.4 above is the idea that sources should be examined for quality before using them. As more and more information becomes available, the range in quality—from treasure to trash—seems to be growing wider. It is increasingly important, then, to apply some effective criteria to the evaluation of each potential source you encounter. Here is one set, known as the EAR test, for Expertise, Accuracy, and Reliability.

3.4.1 Expertise.

The first check of a source should relate to the author's credentials. Is the author an authority in the area, an expert? If not, is the author at least well informed about the area and aware of all the relevant issues? If there is a corporate author, is the organization widely respected or an authority? Does the way the author handles the subject indicate that he or she is knowledgeable, reasonable, and a careful thinker? Often, an institutional affiliation will indicate an expert source. For example, a page on the Web site of a chemical manufacturer describing how to mix ingredients to make shampoo should be highly authoritative.

> **The expertise test:** Is there evidence that the source knows the subject?

3.4.2 Accuracy.

The next check of a source should relate to accuracy, which includes two parts. First is the currency of the information. Is the information up-to-date? In some areas (technology, business), information becomes outdated rapidly. In other areas (some historical work and literary scholarship), the information remains accurate for long periods. Outdated information can be worse than no information because it can be misleading. Check the date of the source and the date of the information in the source to be sure the information is recent enough for your needs.

The second part of accuracy relates to correctness: Are the facts right, the essential details present, the presentation unbiased, the whole picture presented? Be careful of sources that describe everything in sweeping generalizations and that lack details. Sources that ignore conflicting evidence or arguments should be used cautiously, if at all.

> **The accuracy test:** Is the information correct today?

A note on biased sources: There are many areas of controversy, not just in politics, religion, and philosophy, but in science and social science as well, where at least some of your sources will be somewhat or even highly biased. You can use biased sources, as long as you are aware of the bias and seek out opposing viewpoints (which may be biased as well).

3.4.3 Reliability.

The reliability test begins with a look at the source's documentation (bibliography) to see whether the information is well supported. Some sources will have little documentation because the material is a reasoned argument or a report on an original study or empirical investigation. Usually, though, there will be at least some indication of what other books and articles the authors made use of or recommend for further reading.

Another part of the reliability test concerns how well the information in the source correlates with that in other sources. Corroboration—one source supporting or agreeing with another—is one way to test the credibility of information. The belief is that in matters of fact or data-based conclusions, a source that agrees with other sources is more likely to be correct than a source that does not agree. A good practice, then, is to triangulate your sources: Find three sources that agree on important information. This test is not infallible, for the three sources could be all wrong and the fourth, conflicting source could be correct. Nevertheless, the test is generally a good guideline.

> **The reliability test:** Is the information supported by other sources?

3.5 Working with sources that disagree or conflict.

In Chapter 1, Section 1.2.5, it was mentioned that the use of sources that conflict with your position can strengthen your research paper. For this reason, you will want to locate and include some of these sources in your work whenever possible. This section contains advice about how to make use of them.

3.5.1 Identify the source of disagreement.

Whatever subject you research, you are likely to encounter conflicting claims about facts and events themselves or about the meaning of facts and events. In order for you to choose which claims to accept and which to counter with other arguments, you should first locate the source of the conflict. Here are some reasons why sources conflict:

♦ **One source is outdated.** New facts may have come to light, new technological discoveries may have been made, or a new understanding may have arisen. For example, the account of a historical event may be changed when an old manuscript is discovered, explaining how the event occurred. New discoveries in biochemistry change our views of mental illness and treatment. Technical discoveries in computers and digital cameras quickly render even recent information obsolete.

♦ **The sources begin with different assumptions.** Assumptions, often unstated by the writer, underlie much of what is presented. People differ about what constitutes good or acceptable evidence, and what can be assumed without examination.

♦ **The sources are using different definitions.** When a term has no fixed or universal definition, scholars must create a working definition—called a stipulative definition—which serves a specific purpose. When these definitions vary widely from scholar to scholar, the arguments and conclusions of a study or interpretive article can also vary widely. For example, terms such as *mental illness*, *binge drinking*, and *toxic waste* are open to widely different definitions. Thus, if one study claims that there are a thousand toxic waste sites in the United States, while another claims that there are ten thousand or a hundred thousand, the different definitions used by each author may be the source of the disparity.

♦ **Interpretations differ.** This may be the most common reason for conflict in sources. Several people examine a set of facts and create different explanations for those facts. (Indeed, a recommended exercise in problem solving involves creating several explanations for the same set of data. The problem solver can then examine these rival hypotheses to determine which tells the most convincing story.) The meaning of facts is frequently uncertain or ambiguous, so that equally careful and unbiased investigators can quite rationally come to very different conclusions. It is important to remember this fact:

> ## Honest people can differ.

For example, imagine the investigation of a crime scene. All the evidence may be present to the investigators, yet there are, at least initially, several equally plausible explanations.

♦ **The source authors have different values.** Values shape the choices of all of us. Decision making is a product of the available alternatives, the criteria we want our choice to meet, and the values we hold about the worth of each criterion. Analysis and interpretation are in a sense acts of decision making, so they, too, are shaped by our values. A writer who argues that building a dam across a river is a good idea because it will supply electricity and a writer who argues that the dam is a bad idea because of its environmental impact are using the same facts to come to opposite conclusions because their values differ.

♦ **Personal bias is present.** There are many varieties of bias or ideological commitment in every arena of learning. Some people value political agendas over truth. Some have strong commitments to particular viewpoints. For example, a writer who believes that most large corporations are corrupt will write an analysis of a paper shortage with different conclusions from a writer who believes that most large corporations are honest. For some writers, the government is the problem, while for others, the government is the solution. Because bias is often exhibited by an unrepresentative selection of facts, together with a slanted interpretation, two conflicting positions may both appear to be based on evidence.

Of course, these causes are often found in combination. For example, a literary critic who believes that a novelist's personal biography is irrelevant to the meaning of the novel will probably differ from a critic who believes that the novelist's biography is relevant. The resulting articles (or books) would differ because of different assumptions, values, and interpretations.

One important task to perform before you separate your research materials into supporting and opposing sources is to remember this:

> ## The opposing source may be right.

Give some serious thought to the arguments and evidence in the conflicting sources both before and while you write your first draft. Even if you do not ultimately change your position entirely, you may find yourself altering your views to some extent. In other words, avoid falling into *either-or* thinking where you view sources merely as friend or foe. Allow a generous consideration of each viewpoint before you decide on the position you wish to take.

3.5.2 Criticizing opposing sources.

At the places in your research paper where it becomes useful to introduce an opposing or conflicting source, you should provide an effective but fair response to the source. The response will depend on the reason for the conflict. Here are some possible strategies for criticizing a source:

- **An error of fact.** Point out the deficiency in the facts presented by the conflicting source. There are three possibilities. (1) The facts are outdated and have been superceded by newer knowledge. (2) The facts are inaccurate (they may be partially right and partially wrong), confused, or otherwise incorrect. (3) Not all the facts have been taken into account and the source's argument involves incomplete evidence.

- **A weakness in interpretation.** Point out the reason for the difference in interpretation and show why your interpretation is stronger (or why the conflicting interpretation is weak). Reasons for differing interpretations are several. (1) The interpretations are based on different assumptions. (2) The interpretations derive from different values. (3) The source is biased (be careful and fair in showing how). (4) There is an honest difference in the meaning of the data or evidence.

- **Failure to include a significant argument or fact.** Conclusions based on incomplete evidence or evidence selected in a biased way are open to criticism by arguing that if the additional evidence had been included, the conclusion would likely have been different. You may have read arguments where respondents to an argument say, "But this fails to take into account the fact that —," or, "But this argument ignores the issue of —." One caution is relevant here, however. Take care that the omitted argument is truly significant or central to the issue. An unimportant objection raised this way may actually weaken your position rather than the source's because it will appear to be frivolous. (A story tells us that

41

whenever one individual objected to an argument, he would dismiss it with a huff and the comment, "But this argument fails to mention cheese." It was true, but ridiculous.)

♦ **A weak or unacceptable definition.** Occasionally, a writer will create a definition that is too inclusive, too exclusive, or in some other way not acceptable. One type of unacceptable definition commits the fallacy of *begging the question*: The definition is written so that it presents a conclusion or eliminates the consideration of an opposing argument. For example, "I define *mental processes* as those thoughts of which we are consciously aware. Therefore, by definition, there is no such thing as unconscious mental processes."

♦ **An error of reasoning.** Point out the error or fallacy. Possibilities include the following. (1) A conclusion commits the fallacy of *hasty generalization*: generalizing from too little evidence or evidence that is not representative. (2) Another fallacy of reasoning has been committed. See Section 3.5.3 below for some examples. (3) The assumptions behind the argument are incorrect or objectionable.

♦ **Faulty methodology.** Professionals often criticize studies on this basis. Point out flaws in the source of data, the failure of the data to be representative, a flaw in the design of the study, or an error made during the conduct of the investigation.

3.5.3 Avoid criticizing a source unfairly.

When you respond to the arguments that oppose your position in a paper, there are several logical fallacies you should be careful to avoid. Fallacies are errors of reasoning that divert the argument from its proper focus. These fallacies occur most often when writers attack conflicting sources:

♦ *Argumentum ad hominem*: attacking the writer personally rather than arguing against the writer's ideas. For example, "No one but an ignorant fanatic would make such an objection." In that case, responding to the objection logically with good evidence should be easy, so why resort to name calling?

♦ **Genetic error:** rejecting an idea because of its origin. For example, "That remedy for gout has no status because it comes from folk medicine rather than modern science." The issue should not be where it came from but whether or not it works.

♦ **Appeal to prestige:** using a person's or organization's fame as a substitute for evidence or argument. For example, "These findings clearly disprove the objection because they came from a Presidential task force." A good reputation (such as scholarly prestige) adds to the credibility of an argument, but no amount of fame should ever be a substitute for an argument or evidence. To claim superiority for one view over another based on which side has the more famous advocates is sometimes called a *beauty contest*.

♦ **Straw man:** presenting an opposing position or evidence in such an unfair or exaggerated way that it is easy to refute. For example, "Those who advocate raising the speed limit believe that the thousands of additional traffic deaths that would result are an acceptable cost for getting them to their hot tubs five minutes faster." Caricaturing or misrepresenting an opposing viewpoint is not merely unfair to the opponent; the act also diminishes your own credibility and hence the convincing power of your argument. When someone does a "hatchet job" on a conflicting source, readers know it.

◆ **Emotive language:** using emotionally loaded words to stir up the reader's feelings instead of appealing to reason. For example, instead of presenting arguments or evidence to show why a proposal is weak or unworkable, the fallacious writer might say, "This stupid idea will take us back to the nineteenth century. What a bunch of stinking, rotting garbage." Notice that we learn nothing from these comments about the merits (or lack of merits) of the proposal.

Review questions.

To see how well you understand this chapter, attempt to answer each of the following questions without referring to the text. (Write down your answers to make checking easier.) Then check your answers with the text. If you missed something important, add it to your answer.

1. What is the doctrine of *fair use*?

2. In addition to facts, what other kinds of information will be useful to include in a research paper?

3. Distinguish between primary and secondary sources. Give examples.

4. How does quoting a standard dictionary definition weaken a paper?

5. What are some techniques for locating high-quality information on the Internet?

6. Explain the importance of evaluating sources.

7. What are some reasons that sources may conflict?

8. What does it mean to say, "Honest people can differ"?

9. What are some strategies for criticizing an opposing source?

10. What are logical fallacies, and how are they unfair?

Questions for thought and discussion.

Use these questions for in-class discussion or for stimulating your own thinking.

1. When you write a paper, how do you organize your materials (note cards, data files, folders, etc.)? How effective do you find this method and why?

2. Have you ever needed to look up a source a second time in order to write down all or part of its bibliographic information? How much extra time did you spend? Was it frustrating?

3. Have you ever found a source that you initially viewed as a conflicting source to be criticized, only later on to conclude that the source held the superior view or interpretation? If so, explain how your thinking changed.

4. Librarians and other educators have discovered that many students do not distinguish between the types of information they retrieve on a computer screen because the presentation looks so similar. For these students, an anonymous Web page and a refereed journal article are viewed as having the same reliability. How careful are you to think about the variety, nature, and quality of the information you retrieve from electronic sources? Do you usually try to determine the origin and quality of the information you have located?

5. When you research, are you more likely to use the first sources you locate, or do you make an attempt to select carefully from a larger set of possibilities? Why?

6. Have you ever written a research paper where you knew the position you wanted to take before you started? If so, what effect did that have on your selection and evaluation of sources? Were you biased? Did you change your position based on the evidence you found? Explain.

7. When you finish a paper, what steps do you take to ensure the accuracy of your grammar, spelling, punctuation, and so forth?

8. If your school or college has a writing center or similar resource for students who are writing research papers, have you visited it? What kinds of help did you receive? Did the advice you received improve your paper?

Name _____   Course _____

Chapter 3 Review: True-false quiz.

Directions: In each case, determine whether the statement is true or false.

1. The appearance of information in printed form is an indicator of its accuracy.
   ☐ True   ☐ False

2. A source that disagrees with your own conclusions can still be useful in your paper.
   ☐ True   ☐ False

3. Everything posted on the Web is indexed by the better search engines.
   ☐ True   ☐ False

4. In this electronic age, there is no good reason to print out or photocopy any of your sources.
   ☐ True   ☐ False

5. The Declaration of Independence is an example of a primary source.
   ☐ True   ☐ False

6. The reliability of information sometimes suffers when the primary goal is to make the information entertaining.
   ☐ True   ☐ False

7. Beginning a paper with a quotation from a dictionary is a good way to make a favorable impression on your reader.
   ☐ True   ☐ False

8. An important consideration for the EAR test of source evaluation (Expertise, Accuracy, and Reliability) is whether or not there is a date on a Web page you might use.
   ☐ True   ☐ False

9. If two sources present differing conclusions about the same issue, one of them must be factually incorrect.
   ☐ True   ☐ False

10. Sources that oppose your central idea are best handled by ignoring them.
    ☐ True   ☐ False

Name _____   Course _____

Chapter 3 Review: Logical fallacies.

Directions: Identify the logical fallacy committed by each of the following statements.

1. This so-called argument is a bunch of junk—just a lot of empty babble without a bit of significance.
   a. *argumentum ad hominem*
   b. appeal to prestige
   c. straw man
   d. hasty generalization
   e. emotive language

2. The advocates of this plan would have us believe in an infinite stream of money, effectively buying one permanent solution after another without ever a single complication.
   a. *argumentum ad hominem*
   b. appeal to prestige
   c. straw man
   d. hasty generalization
   e. emotive language

3. This opinion comes from a medical doctor at the International Research Institute, so it must be true.
   a. *argumentum ad hominem*
   b. appeal to prestige
   c. straw man
   d. hasty generalization
   e. emotive language

4. Of course, with his mediocre education, Doe was unable to get a job at a first-tier university, and this fact shows us what to make of his theory.
   a. *argumentum ad hominem*
   b. appeal to prestige
   c. straw man
   d. hasty generalization
   e. emotive language

5. After interviews with sixteen subjects taking the economics course, we have concluded that lack of life experience prevents any college student from understanding interest rate fluctuations.
   a. *argumentum ad hominem*
   b. appeal to prestige
   c. straw man
   d. hasty generalization
   e. emotive language

4

Working with Sources

I quote others only to express myself better.
    —Michel de Montaigne

In this chapter, you will learn to work with the sources you have selected. As you read each source, you will want to take notes about important points and then select passages for possible quotation, paraphrase, or summary.

♦ Taking careful notes will make working with sources easier.

♦ Knowing when to quote, paraphrase, and summarize will help you prepare your sources for use.

♦ Learning how to paraphrase and summarize properly will help you avoid plagiarism.

4.1 Taking careful notes.

A major source of confusion, inaccuracy—and sometimes plagiarism—lies in improper note-taking practices. Students who include quotations, summaries, paraphrases, and their own analyses in their reading notes, without clearly distinguishing among those different kinds of information, create difficulties for themselves. Following are some suggestions that will enable you to take careful notes.

4.1.1 Use a labeling system.

Make use of a system or technique for labeling the nature of the various kinds of notes you write down: quotations, comments by you, paraphrases, or summaries. Then when you are making notes as you read a book or article, apply the technique as you read. The goal is to distinguish clearly what each note represents. These distinctions will also enable you to work more quickly because the meaning of each note will always be clear.

♦ **Include the full bibliographic citation** at the beginning of your notes so that subsequent references can be by author and page number or some other shortened format. See Examples 4.1.1.1 and 4.1.1.2 on the next page.

♦ **Use quotation marks around all word-for-word copying,** and include a clear citation. If you take notes by hand, use a large, exaggerated size for the quotation marks to make them clearly visible.

♦ **Label paraphrases with a circled** *P* or other distinguishing mark. When you turn the text into your own words in a paraphrase, you may at a later time confuse it with your own ideas unless it is clearly labeled. Include a citation.

♦ **Label summaries with a circled** *S* or other distinguishing mark. Summaries reduce the material to a shorter form in your own words, so they can be confused with your own work unless they are clearly labeled. Once again, remember to include a citation.

◆ **Label your own ideas with the word *Mine*.** When you add commentary, analysis, or simply write down an idea that occurred to you as you read, circle that writing and attach a label. Your ideas are valuable. Protect them.

Example 4.1.1.1
Sample Notes
Quoted text with bibliographic citation: book, APA style:
Doe, J. (2002). *Tracking subatomic particles*. New York: Physics Press.
"The question remains: Are quarks the fundamental building blocks of matter, or is there something smaller?" page 261
"There are perhaps 100 quintillion atoms in a grain of sand, and yet matter is mostly space." page 144

Quoted text with bibliographic citation: book, MLA style:
Doe, John. *Tracking Subatomic Particles*. New York: Physics Press, 2002.
"The question remains: Are quarks the fundamental building blocks of matter, or is there something smaller?" page 261
"There are perhaps 100 quintillion atoms in a grain of sand, and yet matter is mostly space." page 144

Example 4.1.1.2
Sample Notes
Quoted text with bibliographic citation: article, APA style:
Doe, J. (2003). "A new test for blood evidence." *Journal of Forensic Science, 22*, 265-274.
"The use of Luminol can be problematic because it can produce false positives for blood and damage real blood." page 266

Quoted text with bibliographic citation: article, MLA style:
Doe, Jane. "A New Test for Blood Evidence." *Journal of Forensic Science* 22 (2003): 265-74.
"The use of Luminol can be problematic because it can produce false positives for blood and damage real blood." page 266

Comment: Note that the bibliographic citation for the article includes the beginning and ending page numbers of the article.

If you take notes by hand, you can be creative by using different ink colors to distinguish among the kinds of notes (such as red for quotations, green for paraphrases, blue for summaries, and black for your own ideas), or you can draw boxes or shapes around the text and add labels. If you take notes on a computer, you can use different fonts, different colors of text, or boxes and labels to mark the different kinds of information. Not only do you want to be careful to identify and give credit to your source when you use it, but you also want to be sure that you do not accidentally give your source credit for your own thinking. Your ideas are important.

4.1.2 Quote exactly.

If you are working with physical documents, where you must transcribe the words by handwriting, typing, or even scanning using optical character recognition software, there is a chance for errors to enter the text. Even copying and pasting from an electronic source can introduce errors, especially at the beginning and end of the quotation, because words or punctuation marks are sometimes cut off. Double-check to assure that the text has been copied accurately—that all the words, including proper names, are spelled correctly and that no words have been left out. The word *not* is commonly left out when copying manually, and the loss of that word obviously has a critical effect on the meaning of a quotation.

Quoting exactly also means that you are not permitted to change the spelling of any words in the source, even if that spelling is archaic, incorrect, or nonstandard. For example, you may encounter British spellings such as *humour, honour,* or *aluminium.* In such a case, follow the text. If there is an error in your source text, where a word has been left out, do not silently correct the text. You may insert a missing word with brackets [like this]. See the Polishing Your Prose advice in Appendix A for further information on altering text.

Keep a Quotation File

One of the most common reasons given for inadvertent plagiarism is "confusion in my notes." In other words, the writer mixed up quoted material with the writer's own words and was unable to see the difference, resulting in plagiarizing the quoted material. A good way to help protect yourself from this problem is to keep a separate word processing file for quotations that you copy from electronic sources such as the Web or electronic databases. When you use the quoted material, copy it from your file and paste it into your paper (with appropriate citation, of course). By doing that, if there is ever any question about the quotation (or paraphrase or summary), you can look back at the original and make the comparison easily.

4.1.3 Keep copies of each source with your notes.

Stapling a printout or photocopy of a source article or of book pages to the back of your notes about the source will keep the source handy for further reference, for last minute triple-checking of quotations, and for referring to any notes you made in the margins as you read. The printout includes the context of the words around your quotation or other reference, so that you can recheck that your interpretation or other comment is based on an accurate understanding of the source. Further research and thinking may also lead you to use more of the source. In such a case, the entire source is handy. (If you do not keep a copy of a source and have to return to it later, you may need to read the entire article again because you will not be able to rely on the annotations you made earlier.)

4.1.4 Archive your notes.

As you work with your sources and notes, do not throw anything away. When you are finished with a source, put your notes and the copy of the source in a notebook and hold on to it. If your notes are in electronic form and you use them as a source for copying and pasting, or if you add to and delete as you work toward your final paper, keep copies of printouts or copies of earlier versions of your data files. If any confusion should arise—over what is a quotation and what is your own thinking, for example—you will have the earlier version available to you for consultation and clarification. Early versions of notes may also be useful if you decide to change direction in the paper. And, of course, your ability to demonstrate a history of work on your paper will help protect you from a false charge of plagiarism (see Chapter 2, Section 2.5, for more information).

4.2 Quoting.

Using a quotation—someone's exact words—can have a dramatic and powerful effect in your paper, for you are displaying verbatim (word for word) what someone, often an expert, has said about the point you are making.

4.2.1 When to choose quotation.

Direct quotation may be preferable to a summary or paraphrase for any of several reasons. Some of the unique benefits offered by a direct quotation are as follows:

♦ **Expert declaration.** The exact words of an authority are more powerful than a summary or paraphrase of those words, even if the exact words are not remarkable in themselves. When readers can see precisely what an expert says, they can analyze, dwell on, or react to those words without any concern that some meaning has been lost through a paraphrase or summary.

♦ **Direct support.** An effective way to reinforce a point you are making is to supply a quotation that provides support for it. Quotations have a sense of immediacy lacking in paraphrases or summaries. The quotation serves as a second voice, confirming your point.

♦ **Effective language**. The quality of the writer's language may make it highly quotable. Its elegance, clarity, directness, use of metaphor or other imagery, exactness, aptness—any of these may make the words worth quoting because they will add interest to your paper. Having another voice enter the discussion provides variety as well as impact. If the source says something better than you could, consider quoting.

♦ **Historical flavor.** If you make use of a source from many years ago, the style and vocabulary (and even the spelling) may allow a quotation to offer a special zest to your paper. Some writers have a distinctive and commanding style or an engaging use of rhetorical flourish that offers a unique feel to their ideas.

♦ **Specific example.** A source may tell a story, supply an anecdote, or offer a vivid example best presented in the source's own words. Because most anecdotes are condensed and highly sequenced stories, they are almost impossible to paraphrase or summarize without losing their snap or even their meaning.

♦ **Controversial statement.** If the source makes an outrageous or highly controversial claim, quoting the source directly will (1) remove your reader's skepticism about what the source really said and (2) help distance you from responsibility for the idea or the words used to express it.

♦ **Material for analysis.** When you intend to comment on, explain, analyze, or criticize an idea, quoting it places the exact words at issue before the reader for reference as you make your remarks. You can then proceed to quote short phrases or even single words in your analysis without confusing the reader about the context of those words.

4.2.2 Cautions about quoting.

If wisdom is the prudent application of knowledge, then use wisdom when you decide to quote. Here are three unwise uses of quotation:

♦ **Quoting too often.** Too many quotations in a paper will push your ideas into the background and take over the paper, rather than act as a support to your writing. Recall from Chapter 1, Section 1.4.1, that your own thinking is the purpose of the paper; you are not assembling a quotation dictionary. If you explain, discuss, or apply most of your quotations, you should be able to avoid overquotation. The number of quotations considered too many depends upon the nature of the writing project, of course, but it also depends upon how long the quotations are. As you will learn in the next chapter, quotations can range from fairly long to very short. As a rule, short quotations can appear more frequently than long quotations.

♦ **Quoting one source too many times.** Some instructors provide rules of thumb for their research paper assignments, not permitting the quotation (or citation in any form) of one source more than a certain amount. (For example, the rule may be that a student may not use one source more than three times in a 2500-word paper.) Whether you have such a rule or not, the overuse of one source implies too much dependence on it. If the citations from a single source occur one after the other without other intervening citations, and if they are sequential (as in pages 265, 288, and 299), it will appear to the reader that the source is being transferred into the paper wholesale, not integrated and analyzed along with other materials.

♦ **Quoting too long.** For many instructors, a synonym for *lengthy quotation* is *padding* because in many cases that is exactly what is taking place. However, there is another reason for avoiding lengthy quotations: They are ineffective. Many readers have a habit of skipping past long quotations. An occasional four- to six-line quotation might be desirable, but a ten- or twelve-line quotation would need to be quite spectacular to be worth including. See Chapter 6, Section 6.4.1, for further information.

4.2.3 Avoid the fallacy of vicious abstraction.

Vicious abstraction occurs when a quotation takes on a meaning different from that intended by its author because the words are taken out of their surrounding context. Vicious abstraction can occur as a result of several different circumstances:

♦ **The source author is presenting someone else's position.** Many times, writers summarize or paraphrase their opponent's position in order to respond to it later. If a research paper writer quotes from one of these summaries and attributes the views to the source writer, vicious abstraction results because the source writer is *describing* those views, not *advocating* them.

♦ **The source author's words require the source context** for an accurate understanding of the meaning, and quoting the words out of context creates a false impression. Many statements require some context (such as the surrounding paragraph) in order to be fully and accurately understood.

♦ **The research paper writer omits some words from the quotation** (often clearly showing the omission with ellipsis dots), and the abbreviated quotation takes on a meaning different from the full quotation. You are allowed to omit words from a quotation for the sake of eliminating unnecessary language, but the meaning of the quotation must remain the same.

Example 4.2.3.1
Quotation:
The group known as Motorists for Faster Driving argues that higher speed limits will enable us to get to our destinations faster, thus reducing our risk time on the road. In other words, we should raise or eliminate speed limits for safety's sake. Such an argument neglects the fact that higher speed equals higher-speed crashes. —John Doe, 2001, p. 75

Vicious Abstraction, APA style:
Doe (2001) believes that "we should raise or eliminate speed limits for safety's sake" (p. 75).

Comment:
While the words are accurately quoted from Doe, they represent a viewpoint he is describing (and then rejecting) rather than one he is advocating.

Example 4.2.3.2
Quotation:
A little learning is a dang'rous thing;
Drink deep, or taste not the Pierian spring:
There shallow draughts intoxicate the brain,
And drinking largely sobers us again.
    — Alexander Pope

Vicious Abstraction:
Alexander Pope warns us that "learning is a dang'rous thing."

Comment:
Pope's point is that a small amount of learning is dangerous, but that great learning "sobers us" and is therefore beneficial. The vicious abstraction expresses nearly the opposite of Pope's idea.

4.3 Paraphrasing.

Quoting is only one way to incorporate a source's ideas into your research paper. Another way is to paraphrase the source.

4.3.1 What is a paraphrase?

A paraphrase is a restatement or rewriting of a source in order to present the source's idea without actually quoting the source. In other words:

> A paraphrase converts a source's words into about the same number of your own words.

In order to avoid plagiarism, follow these guidelines for a successful paraphrase:

♦ **The paraphrase must be almost entirely in your own words:** new vocabulary (such as synonyms) and new phrases. Do not mix your own words with any of the source's words (unless you quote the source's words). (Of course, you may use the same technical terms, such as *chronic insomnia*, and the same helper words, such as *a, and, the, of, in, is,* and so forth.)

◆ **Use a different sentence structure from that of the source.** Recast the ideas into your own presentation. Do not copy the arrangement of clauses or other rhetorical structures.

◆ **In most cases, rearrange the order of the ideas.** You must include all of the points and ideas of the source, but you should rearrange or reconvey them. For passages that require a specific sequence, such as scientific processes, historical events, or cause-and-effect descriptions, maintain the order of the source at the major steps. You still may wish to rearrange the discussion within each step.

◆ **Put quotation marks around any exact words you retain** from the source. Quoting particularly effective phrases from the source is not technically part of a paraphrase, but doing so can lend flavor and sparkle to the paraphrase. Just be sure to include quotation marks around each phrase you quote.

◆ **Provide a citation** that clearly gives credit to the source for the ideas in the paraphrase.

In order to create a paraphrase that is ethical and appropriate, follow these guidelines:

◆ **Use the same number of words.** Keep the paraphrase about the same number of words as the original, not omitting any significant features of the source material. Include each point, major and minor, from the original.

◆ **Preserve the meaning.** Take care to preserve the author's original meaning and to avoid taking the ideas out of context. What the author stressed as the main points of the passage should be kept as the main points of the paraphrase.

4.3.2 When to paraphrase.

Any one of several conditions can make paraphrasing a good choice as a means of incorporating a source into your paper:

◆ **Arrangement for emphasis.** The rearrangement of ideas and sentence structure associated with the process of paraphrasing allows you to emphasize the ideas of importance to your paper. The end of a sentence or passage has the most emphasis, the beginning the second most, and the middle the least. Therefore, if your source mentions an idea in the middle of a long sentence, your paraphrase can position the idea at the end, giving it more impact.

◆ **Simplifying the material.** The material may need to be simplified either in sentence structure, vocabulary, or presentation. The source may be highly technical or specific to a particular discipline, while you may be writing for a more general audience. The complexity of the argument may make it difficult to follow. In such cases, you can simplify the material through a paraphrase. The act of paraphrasing will increase your own understanding of the source material, and the paraphrase itself will increase your reader's understanding.

◆ **Clarifying the material.** The material can be presented more clearly because the source has a complex style or technical vocabulary. Some brilliant thinkers write poorly. Others encumber their writing with an excess of jargon, overuse the passive voice, or otherwise render their words less effective than their ideas. Paraphrasing under these circumstances is useful. Quoting a source your reader cannot understand will not help your paper, but providing a clear paraphrase will.

♦ **Normalizing your paper's style.** The style and comprehension level of the paper should be kept consistent. In constructing your research paper, you may use sources from the highly sophisticated to the simple, while you may want to maintain a uniform style and reading level. In such a case, paraphrasing sources allows you to convert them into your own style and vocabulary.

♦ **Keeping the same length.** If the length of the source does not need to be shortened (as a summary would do), or more details are desired than a summary would provide, a paraphrase is the right choice.

4.3.3 How to paraphrase.

To create an effective paraphrase, follow these steps:

♦ **Read the source passage several times.** In order to get a complete understanding of the passage, read it over more than once. Consult a dictionary, if necessary, to define any words you do not know. Use your reading comprehension skills here: Read the passage, look away, think about what you just read, recite out loud what you think the passage means, and then check your understanding by looking at the passage again. This first step is crucial, for you cannot paraphrase a passage accurately if you do not understand it.

♦ **Outline the passage.** Use your own words and phrases for writing the outline so that you can be free to use them as the building blocks of your paraphrase. You might write the first version of the outline without consulting the passage, in order to avoid the temptation of borrowing words or phrases from it. Then, consult the passage again to ensure that the outline is accurate and complete. Remember that a paraphrase does not omit any ideas.

♦ **Rearrange the outline.** Change the order of items to reflect the order of emphasis you want to present in your paraphrase or to create better clarity. For example, the author may present a conclusion at the beginning of the passage, while you may want to put it at the end of your paraphrase. (Keep in mind the exceptions mentioned in Section 4.3.1.)

♦ **Write the paraphrase.** Use the outline or your memory to write the paraphrase. Do not look at the source text.

♦ **Check the result.** Compare the paraphrase with the original to be sure that you have preserved the source's meaning accurately. Be sure you have not accidentally included exact words or phrases you remembered from reading the source. (The technical term for this is *cryptomnesia*, inadvertently forgetting where you read phrases and thinking that they are your own.)

♦ **Add the appropriate citation.** A good idea is to include a possible lead-in as well, so that your paraphrase is appropriately introduced. Be sure the source is properly credited, using the citation style you have chosen or been assigned.

When you are finished, double-check the guidelines in Section 4.3.1 to be sure they have been satisfied. Study the following examples to help you understand the process.

Example 4.3.3.1

Source text:

Invention, strictly speaking, is little more than a new combination of those images which have been previously gathered and deposited in the memory: nothing can come of nothing: he who has laid up no materials, can produce no combinations. —Sir Joshua Reynolds, *Discourses on Art*, 1797/1965, pp. 15-16

Outline using your own words:
(1) Creativity combines ideas or visual impressions already remembered.
(2) Everything needs a source or original.
(3) Without ideas or images, there is no raw material to intermix.

Rearrange:
(3) Without a stock of ideas, there is no raw material to intermix to get a new product.
(2) Everything needs a source.
(1) Creativity in painting [thus] is an act of combining visual impressions seen and remembered.

Write using APA style of citation:

Reynolds (1797/1965) tells us that without a stock of ideas, the artist will have no raw material to intermix to get a new idea because every creation needs a source. Creativity in painting is therefore an act of combining visual impressions the artist has seen and remembered (pp. 15-16).

Write using MLA style of citation:

Sir Joshua Reynolds tells us that without a stock of ideas, the artist will have no raw material to intermix to get a new idea because every creation needs a source. Creativity in painting is therefore an act of combining visual impressions the artist has seen and remembered (15-16).

Comments:

Note here that the original quotation contains 39 words, while the paraphrase has 44. The ideas are all included, while the language is clarified and the concept of creativity ("invention" in the original) is placed last for emphasis.

Example 4.3.3.2

Source text:

Historically, the quality of a decision has corresponded directly with the quantity of information resources available for making the decision. However, today the explosive increase in the quantity of information has created a new reality, that when a certain point is reached, referred to as information overload, the amount of information is such that it reduces the quality of the decision because the information can no longer be effectively processed. Thus, the overabundance of information actually inhibits rather than enhances decision quality. —John Doe, 2001, p. 123

Outline using your own words:
(1) In the past (or until recently), a better decision came from a larger amount of information.
(2) But now the amount of information is increasing so much that it can make decisions worse.
(3) Called information overload when too much information cannot all be taken into account.

(4) So too much information can hurt rather than improve a decision.

Rearrange:
(3) Called information overload when too much information cannot all be taken into account.
(1) In the past (or until recently), a better decision came from a larger amount of information.
(2) But now the amount of information is increasing so much that it can make decisions worse.
(4) So too much information can hurt rather than improve a decision.

Write using APA style of citation:
As Doe (2001) tells us, information overload occurs when so much information is present that it cannot all be taken into account. In the past, the more information available for making a decision, the better the decision would be. Today, however, there is so much information available for making most decisions that a point can be reached where acquiring still more information can be harmful. An attempt to take too much information into account hurts rather than helps the resulting decision (p. 123).

Write using MLA style of citation:
As John Doe tells us, information overload occurs when so much information is present that it cannot all be taken into account. In the past, the more information available for making a decision, the better the decision would be. Today, however, there is so much information available for making most decisions that a point can be reached where acquiring still more information can be harmful. An attempt to take too much information into account hurts rather than helps the resulting decision (123).

Comments:
The source text has been rearranged to emphasize the concept of information overload and to simplify the vocabulary and sentence structure. Length is comparable, with the source being 73 words and the paraphrase 76 words.

Example 4.3.3.3
Source text:
Retailers may use discounted-price sales in order to clear excess inventories. However, if price discounting occurs too frequently, customers might come to expect such events regularly and therefore defer purchases in anticipation of upcoming off-price events. In such a case, this shifted buying pattern will reduce the retailer's full-margin volume and possibly only worsen the excess inventory problem. —Jane Doe, 2003, p. 321

Outline using your own words:
(1) Some stores have regular lower-price sales to reduce the oversupply of merchandise.
(2) If there are too many sales, customers will begin to take them for granted.
(3) Customers will then put off buying from the store until a sale is on.
(4) This behavior will lower the number of goods sold at full price.
(5) These lower sales may increase the oversupply of merchandise.

Rearrange:
(1) Some stores have regular lower-price sales to reduce the oversupply of merchandise.
(5) These lower sales may increase the oversupply of merchandise.
(3) Customers will then put off buying from the store until a sale is on.
(2) If there are too many sales, customers will begin to take them for granted.

(4) This behavior will lower the number of goods sold at full price.

Write using APA style citation:
Some stores, according to Doe (2003), employ regular lower-price sales in order to reduce the oversupply of merchandise on hand, but this practice can actually increase the oversupply. When sales occur too often, customers will wait for a sale before buying because they take the sale opportunities for granted. This behavior will lower the number of goods sold at full price, leaving them in inventory (p. 321).

Write using MLA style citation:
Some stores, according to Jane Doe, employ regular lower-price sales in order to reduce the oversupply of merchandise on hand, but this practice can actually increase the oversupply. When sales occur too often, customers will wait for a sale before buying because they take the sale opportunities for granted. This behavior will lower the number of goods sold at full price, leaving them in inventory (321).

Comments:
The source text has been rearranged to highlight the unintended effects of too-frequent sales on inventory. Sentences (2) and (3) have been intermixed in the paraphrase. As with the other examples above, note that the writer is free to improve, add, and delete words from the outline, even though the outline is written in complete sentences, paraphrasing each source sentence. Length of the two passages is comparable, with the source at 58 words and the paraphrase at 61.

4.3.4 Cautions about paraphrasing.

When you create your paraphrase, take care to avoid the most common errors of paraphrasing:

- **Changing only some of the words.** Writers who change only a few words or who include various phrases from the source in the paraphrase commit plagiarism. As the instructions above note, all of the words must be different (other than technical terms under discussion, such as *information overload* and the helper words, such as *the, and, of*, etc.).
- **Changing words but keeping the same sentence structure and order of presentation.** Paraphrasing must be more than substituting synonyms for every word in the original. Rewrite the source.
- **Adding ideas or explanation.** The paraphrase should reflect the source accurately, and must not include ideas absent from the source. Explanation of the paraphrase should come in your own subsequent discussion, not in the paraphrase itself.
- **Adding interpretation or assessment.** The paraphrase should not include your evaluation or judgment of the ideas. Evaluate afterwards. Avoid also any biased presentation of the meaning, such as the use of emotive, belittling, or sarcastic words in the paraphrase. Rise above such unjust tactics.
- **Creating a straw man fallacy.** Writers who exaggerate or misrepresent the source in a way that makes it an easier target for rebuttal commit the straw man fallacy. Take care that your paraphrase is fair, especially if you are hostile toward the source. See Example 4.3.4.1 below and Chapter 3, Section 3.5.3.

Example 4.3.4.1

Source:

Unless steps are taken to provide a predictable and stable energy supply in the face of growing demand, the nation may be in danger of sudden power losses or even extended blackouts, thus damaging our industrial and information-based economies. Building more gas-fired generation plants seems to be the best answer. —John Doe, 2002, p. 231

Fair paraphrase:

Doe (2002) believes that we must construct additional power plants fueled by natural gas if we are to have a reliable electricity supply during this period of increasing usage. Without that, the country's economic base (both industrial and information-driven) may be damaged by lengthy blackouts or abrupt losses of power (p. 231).

Inadequate paraphrase:

Doe (2002) recommends that the government take action **to provide a predictable and stable energy supply** because of constantly **growing demand**. Otherwise, we may be in danger of losing power or even experiencing **extended blackouts**. These circumstances could **damage our industrial and information-based economy**. He says that **gas-fired plants** appear **to be the best answer** (p. 231).

Comment:

The writer of this inadequate paraphrase commits plagiarism by including many word-for-word phrases from the source (indicated by the bold type). The order of the ideas is also unchanged from the source. Changing only a few words in a source creates an inadequate paraphrase because it plagiarizes the remainder of the source.

Straw man fallacy paraphrase:

Doe claims that if we do not litter the whole country with a bunch of heavily polluting power plants, there is no way to ensure a reliable supply of power in the face of constantly growing wasteful usage. Without all those new plants, he alleges, our whole economy will collapse, and we will all be cast into permanent darkness (p. 231).

Comment:

The straw man paraphrase is not only a mischaracterization of Doe, attributing extremist claims to him ("economy will collapse," "permanent darkness"), but it also uses highly emotive terms to sneer at the writer and his argument ("claims," "litter," "alleges"). Interpretations of the facts are also added to the paraphrase ("heavily polluting," "wasteful"). Remember that the place to attack a position you reject is *after* you have presented the author's position as accurately as you can.

4.4 Summarizing.

In addition to quoting and paraphrasing, your third choice for incorporating a source is to summarize it.

4.4.1 What is a summary?

A summary is a condensed restatement or rewriting of a source in order to present the source's idea in a more focused or shorter way than quoting or paraphrasing would allow. In other words:

A summary reduces a source's words into fewer of your own words.

In order to avoid plagiarism, follow these guidelines for a successful summary:

- **The summary must be almost entirely in your own words:** new vocabulary (such as synonyms) and new phrases. Do not mix your own words with any of the source's words (unless you quote the source's words). (Once again, you may use the same technical terms and helper words.)
- **Use a sentence structure different from that of the source.** Recast the ideas into your own presentation.
- **Rearrange the order of the ideas.** A summary will omit some ideas, but the remaining ones should be reordered as well. (If you are summarizing a passage describing a process or necessary sequence of events, you may maintain the order of the source.)
- **Use quotation marks** around any exact words you retain from the source.
- **Provide a citation** that clearly gives the source credit for the ideas.

In order to create a summary that is ethical and appropriate, take care to preserve the author's original meaning and to avoid taking the ideas out of context.

4.4.2 When to summarize.

The power of summarizing comes from its flexibility. A summary can shorten a source text moderately or dramatically, depending on your application. You may want to reduce a section from a book or article to about a third or a fourth of its original length, or you may want to summarize an entire article or even a book in a paragraph. A summary at its most condensed might involve only a single word or two. For example, if you have just presented an argument for a position, quoting and citing a source or two, you might continue to bolster your case by referring briefly to other sources that also argue in favor of your position: "This view is also supported by Jones (2001), Smith (1998), and Doe (2004)." Here you have summarized each of these three sources by stating that they are in agreement with your argument. A summary has several uses:

- **Simplify the source.** An argument or discussion that may take several pages in the source can be condensed, clarified, and simplified.
- **Eliminate the extras.** Unneeded examples, digressions, or explanations can be omitted, keeping only the main points or the main argument.
- **Condense the source.** Fewer details are needed than a paraphrase would provide. A summary can be a more general statement of the overall meaning of the source.
- **Make a minor point.** A source contributes to your argument in a minor way, or you wish to refer to it only briefly.

4.4.3 How to summarize.

To create an effective summary, follow these steps:

- **Read the source passage several times.** In order to get a complete understanding of the passage, read it over more than once. Consult a dictionary, if necessary, to define any word you do not know. Use your reading comprehension skills here: Read the passage, look away, think about what you just read, recite out loud what you think the passage means, and then check your understanding by looking at the passage again. This first step is crucial because you cannot summarize a passage accurately if you do not understand it.

♦ **Decide how long a summary you need.** Depending on your purpose, you may need a paragraph, a few sentences, one sentence, or part of a sentence. Keeping the length goal in mind will guide you in the remaining steps.

♦ **Outline the passage.** Use your own words and phrases for writing the outline so that you can be free to use them as the building blocks of your summary. As you outline, include the main points, but omit the supporting material you do not need. Be careful, however, not to alter the meaning. If the source is short enough, you might attempt to write the outline without consulting the source, in order to avoid the temptation of borrowing words or phrases from it. Then check to be sure you have included all the main ideas.

♦ **Rearrange the outline.** Change the order of the outline to reflect the order of emphasis you want to present in the summary.

♦ **Write the summary.** Use the outline to guide you, and do not look at the source text.

♦ **Check the result.** Compare the summary with the original to be sure that you have accurately preserved the source's meaning. Be sure that you have not accidentally included exact words or phrases you remembered from reading the source, or if you have, be sure to put quotation marks around them.

♦ **Add the appropriate citation.** In addition to crediting the source properly, you might also want to include an appropriate lead-in to the summary. You might not use exactly that lead-in for the final paper, but it will provide a possibility.

Example 4.4.3.1
Source text:
Fire is both a devastating and a renewing event in the life of the forest. An unchecked forest fire can clear thousands of acres, burning to ashes every tree, bush, and vine, together with the plant material on the forest floor that supplies mulch for vegetation, protection and food for insects, and (along with roots) erosion control. Small animals and insects are killed off by the fire and heat while larger animals that survive temporarily by fleeing may live only to starve later because their food supply has been eliminated. Without the erosion control of the forest plants, the winter rains can wash precious topsoil away, clogging rivers and killing fish and leaving an even more barren landscape. However, the same fire that has caused this destruction also has cleansed the forest of dead or diseased trees and killed harmful pests (such as pine beetles). Some types of seeds require the heat of a fire in order to germinate; they now have the opportunity to begin new life. Other small seedlings are now able to grow also, freed from the deep shade and competition of the previous vegetation. Even the ashes can add their chemistry to the soil. —Jane Doe, 2004, p. 132

Decide the length:
This summary should be one-fourth of the original (therefore, here about 50 words).

Outline using your own words and omitting lesser details:
(1) Fire can harm and help a forest.
(2) Trees, shrubs, dead leaves, and pine needles—all are burned to powder.
(3) Smaller wildlife is killed.

(4) Loss of roots and mulch can cause mudslides.
(5) Unhealthy trees have been purged from the forest by the fire.
(6) Insect pests have also been eliminated.
(7) Seeds that require heat to sprout can grow.
(8) Plants that could not compete with large trees can thrive, also.
(9) Ashes help the soil.

Rearrange:
(2) Trees, shrubs, dead leaves, and pine needles—all are burned to powder.
(4) Loss of roots and mulch can cause mudslides.
(3) Smaller wildlife is killed.
(6) Insect pests have also been eliminated.
(5) Unhealthy trees have been purged from the forest by the fire.
(9) Ashes help the soil.
(7) Seeds that require heat to sprout can grow.
(8) Plants that could not compete with large trees can thrive, also.
(1) Fire can harm and help a forest.

First draft:
In describing the effects of a forest fire, Doe (2004) points out that everything—trees, shrubs, leaves on the ground—is burned to powder, eliminating roots and mulch that would prevent mudslides. Even smaller wildlife is killed. However, she also notes that insect pests are killed as well, together with unhealthy trees. Their ashes have become a soil amendment. Seeds that require heat to sprout can now grow, and plants that would never grow in the deep shade of the forest can now thrive. In Doe's view, then, fire can be both harmful and helpful to a forest (p. 132).

Comment:
This draft has reduced the passage by only 50 percent. You may need to work through several drafts to achieve your length goal, since it is difficult to hit a length target on the first try. Measuring your progress sets up a new goal. Here the new goal is to reduce the first summary draft by half.

Second draft:
In describing the effects of a forest fire, Doe (2004) points out that everything is burned to powder, eliminating both trees and the mulch that would prevent mudslides. Even smaller wildlife is killed. However, she further notes that insect pests are killed, also, together with unhealthy trees, turning their ashes into a soil amendment. Seeds that require heat to sprout can now grow. In Doe's view, then, fire can be both harmful and helpful to a forest (p. 132).

Comment:
This draft contains 75 words. At this point, you may decide that the summary is as condensed as you need it and adopt this version for your paper. If you still want the 50-word version, you can reduce the draft further. Your new goal is to reduce this draft by one-third.

Third draft using APA citation style:
In a forest fire, Doe (2004) points out, everything is destroyed: Trees and mulch turn to ashes, and smaller wildlife is killed. However, she notes that insect pests and unhealthy trees are also turned to a soil-amending ash, while heat-sprouted seeds can now thrive. In Doe's view, then, a forest fire can be both harmful and helpful (p. 132).

Third draft using MLA citation style:
In a forest fire, Jane Doe points out, everything is destroyed: Trees and mulch turn to ashes, and smaller wildlife is killed. However, she notes that insect pests and diseased trees are also turned to a soil-amending ash, while heat-germinating seeds can now grow. In Doe's view, then, a forest fire can be both harmful and helpful (132).

Comment:
This draft is 55 words, close to our goal. When you work on several drafts of a text, hammering it down to fewer and fewer words, not only will you come to know the text itself very well, but you will also gain insights into exactly what you see as the important or even essential parts of the text. In addition, you will develop your writing skills further, as you wrestle with sentence structures and phrasings in an effort to hone down the number of words to meet your requirements. Summarizing can be an exciting challenge.

An alternative technique for summarizing is to construct a sentence outline that contains about the same number of words as the projected summary. In the situation above, for example, the outline would be limited to about 50 words. Writing a summary of the desired length based on the outline then becomes simpler. The challenge in this case lies in trimming down the ideas into an appropriate-length outline. You may wish to experiment to see which of these techniques works better for you.

4.4.4 Cautions about summarizing.

The cautions that apply to paraphrasing also apply to summarizing:

- **Be careful to use your own words and sentence structure** to write the summary.
- **Avoid adding your own ideas to the summary.** Do not fill out assumptions or other unstated ideas.
- **Avoid adding interpretive comments to the summary.** Your comments and interpretation should follow the summary.
- **Be careful to summarize fairly** and avoid creating a straw man fallacy.

See Section 4.3.4 above for detailed information about these cautions. In addition to these, there are two cautions relevant only to summaries:

- **Avoid presenting a minor point in the source as a major point.** When you summarize and omit various details, be careful that a minor point does not appear to be the main point of the passage (or article or book). If necessary, you can indicate a minor point with language such as "covers briefly," "also mentions," "adds that," and so on.
- **Avoid presenting a major point in the source as a minor point.** The omission of details, explanations, and examples can sometimes make a point that was discussed at great length appear less important than other, more minor, points in your summary, unless you are careful. If necessary, you can clarify the difference between major and minor points: "One of Doe's most significant points is—."

Review questions.

To see how well you understand this chapter, attempt to answer each of the following questions without referring to the text. (Write down your answers to make checking easier.) Then check your answers with the text. If you missed something important, add it to your answer.

1. Why should you archive your notes as you construct your research paper?

2. What are the reasons for choosing to quote over choosing to paraphrase?

3. Define the fallacy of vicious abstraction and give an example.

4. Why should you avoid quoting one source several times in a row?

5. Explain what a paraphrase is and how to construct one.

6. Explain what a summary is and how it differs from a paraphrase.

Questions for thought and discussion.

Use these questions for in-class discussion or for stimulating your own thinking.

1. When you write a paper, are you more likely to use one method of source use (quotation, paraphrase, or summary) over another? If so, why?

2. As you take notes, how do you make sure to identify the difference between a quotation and a summary or between a quotation and your own ideas? (In other words, what kind of note-taking system do you use?)

3. Have you ever been told by an instructor that your paper was lost? Did you have a copy? What happened?

4. Have you ever intentionally padded a paper with long quotations or with many quotations? If so, why?

5. Has anyone ever quoted you out of context so that your words were misunderstood? If so, how did you feel? What did you do? Explain.

Name _____   Course _____

Chapter 4 Review: True-false quiz.

Directions: In each case, determine whether the statement is true or false.

1. When working with sources, using a labeling system can help distinguish not only between a quotation and a paraphrase, but also between a source's idea and your own.
   ☐ True   ☐ False

2. Lengthy quotations in a research paper are often ineffective because many readers skip them.
   ☐ True   ☐ False

3. A paraphrase reduces the number of words needed to convey a source's ideas.
   ☐ True   ☐ False

4. You can use some of the source's words in a summary or paraphrase, but only if you put them in quotation marks.
   ☐ True   ☐ False

5. When you summarize, it is a good idea to indicate your attitude toward the source in the summary.
   ☐ True   ☐ False

6. A summary can be as short as a phrase or a sentence.
   ☐ True   ☐ False

7. A full bibliographic citation is an important part of your note-taking and labeling system.
   ☐ True   ☐ False

8. It is **not** a good idea to quote a source whose style and vocabulary are different from modern American usage.
   ☐ True   ☐ False

9. A good way to paraphrase is to use the thesaurus in your word processor to replace the words in your source's sentences with synonyms.
   ☐ True   ☐ False

10. The fallacy of vicious abstraction can occur when a writer mistakenly believes that a source is advocating an idea that the source is merely describing.
    ☐ True   ☐ False

Name _____ Course _____

Chapter 4 Review: Acceptable use or plagiarism?

Directions: Read the source text and then compare it with each of the potential uses that follow. The usage may involve a summary, a paraphrase, or a combination, and may include quotation. In each case ask, "Is the potential use acceptable or does it commit plagiarism?" Explain your answers. (Note: This review uses APA citation style.)

Source text.

To communicate effectively with other people, one must have a reasonably accurate idea of what they do and do not know that is pertinent to the communication. Treating people as though they have knowledge that they do not have can result in miscommunication and perhaps embarrassment. On the other hand, a fundamental rule of conversation, at least according to a Gricean view, is that one generally does not convey to others information that one can assume they already have (Grice, 1975). A speaker who overestimates what his or her listeners know may talk over their heads; one who underestimates their knowledge may, in the interest of being clear, be perceived as talking down to them. Both types of misjudgment work against effective and efficient communication (Nickerson, 1999, p. 737).

Potential use 1.

To communicate effectively, we must have a reasonably accurate idea of what our listeners do and do not know that is pertinent to the communication. Treating people as if they know something they do not can result in miscommunication and perhaps embarrassment. On the other hand, a foundational rule of conversation, at least according to a Gricean view, is that we usually do not convey to others information that we can assume they already have (Grice, 1975). A speaker who overestimates what his or her listeners know may talk over their heads, while someone who underestimates their knowledge may be perceived as talking down to them. Both mistakes work against effective and efficient communication (Nickerson, 1999, p. 737).

☐ Acceptable Use   ☐ Plagiarism

Potential use 2.

For effective communication, it is necessary to have a fairly accurate idea of what our listeners know or do not know that is pertinent to the communication. If we assume that people know something they do not, then miscommunication and perhaps embarrassment may result. At the same time, a fundamental rule of conversation is that we should not convey information that we assume our listeners already have. If our assumption is wrong, we may talk over our listeners' heads, or possibly be perceived as talking down to them. Both errors work against effective and efficient communication (Nickerson, 1999, p. 737).

☐ Acceptable Use   ☐ Plagiarism

Potential use 3.
Nickerson (1999) argues that effective communication depends on a generally accurate knowledge of what the audience knows that "is pertinent to the communication." If a speaker assumes too much knowledge about the subject, the audience will either misunderstand or be bewildered. However, assuming too little knowledge among those in the audience may cause them to feel patronized. In either case, the communication will be less successful than it could have been (p. 737).

☐ Acceptable Use   ☐ Plagiarism

Potential use 4.
As Nickerson (1999) reminds us, "To communicate effectively with other people, one must have a reasonably accurate idea of what they do and do not know that is pertinent to the communication" (p. 737). If we treat people as if they have knowledge that they do not have, we can cause miscommunication and perhaps embarrassment. On the other hand, it is important not to convey to others information that we can assume they already have. A speaker who overestimates what his or her listeners know may talk over their heads, and one who underestimates their knowledge may be perceived as talking down to them. Both of these wrong estimations work against effective and efficient communication.

☐ Acceptable Use   ☐ Plagiarism

Potential use 5.
We are informed by Nickerson (1999), "To communicate effectively with other people, one must have a reasonably accurate idea of what they do and do not know that is pertinent to the communication." It is crucial to assume neither too much nor too little knowledge of the subject by the audience, or the communication may be inhibited by either confusion or offense (p. 737).

☐ Acceptable Use   ☐ Plagiarism

Potential use 6.
If we are to engage in effective communication, we must not talk down to our audience nor talk beyond their understanding. It is therefore very important that we have a generally accurate idea of what our audience knows about the subject.

☐ Acceptable Use   ☐ Plagiarism

5
Putting It Together

Have you ever observed that we pay much more attention to a wise
passage when it is quoted than when we read it in the original author?
—Philip G. Hamerton

Now that you know how to select and prepare your sources for use in your research paper, there remains the task of putting everything together in a way that makes your writing clear and effective. Your sources should be smoothly built into the flow of your paper and yet clearly distinguished from your own writing. This chapter explains how to integrate your sources with your own words.

- ♦ Applying the Simple Rule by marking the boundaries of your source will clearly differentiate your words and ideas from your source's.
- ♦ Using a variety of introductory strategies will make your use of sources more interesting and effective.
- ♦ Knowing how to punctuate quotations will increase the accuracy of your writing.
- ♦ Learning about the variety of ways to quote will give you more choices in the ways you use your sources.

5.1 The Simple Rule: Mark the boundaries.

The Simple Rule for incorporating sources into your writing is *Mark the boundaries.* The rule is a reminder to distinguish carefully between your own words and ideas and those of the sources you use. Simply stated, you place boundary markers around the source material you use to set it off from your own writing. In other words, you indicate clearly when you begin to draw upon a source and when you have finished. The source material is framed or enclosed by the use of boundary markers.

5.1.1 Marking the boundaries of short quotations.

When you use an author's exact words, marking the boundaries involves using quotation marks for quotations of fewer than four lines or about forty words or less. In addition to the quotation marks, the markers include an introductory lead-in and a citation.

Marking the boundaries of short quotations
- ♦ a short phrase or part of a sentence
  - ♦ an entire sentence
- ♦ two or three sentences

Boundaries are marked by a lead-in, opening and closing quotation marks, and a citation.

Example 5.1.1.1
Phrase, APA:
Doe (2004) argues that history is "an interpretation of selected events" rather than a mere presentation of facts (p. 131).

Phrase, MLA:
John Doe argues that history is "an interpretation of selected events" rather than a mere presentation of facts (131).

Example 5.1.1.2
Part of a sentence, APA:
The practice of blood letting to cure disease, writes Doe (2000), was derived from "the medieval theory of the four humours, which supposed that many ailments arose from an excess of blood in need of reducing to its proper level" (p. 224).

Part of a sentence, MLA:
The practice of blood letting to cure disease, writes Jane Doe, was derived from "the medieval theory of the four humours, which supposed that many ailments arose from an excess of blood in need of reducing to its proper level" (224).

Example 5.1.1.3
Entire sentence, APA:
Doe (2003) views the site as a probable burial pit: "The artifacts of the L2 site were all bunched together within a rough circle approximately three meters in diameter" (p. 233).

Entire sentence, MLA:
Doe views the site as a probable burial pit: "The artifacts of the L2 site were all bunched together within a rough circle approximately three meters in diameter" (233).

In all of these examples above, the author's words are clearly marked and attributed to the author. This boundary marking process separates the source information from your own ideas and comments.

5.1.2 Marking the boundaries for long quotations.

When you quote more than four lines or forty words, the quotation is set off from the rest of the text using a block indentation that visually shows the boundaries of the quoted words. Because of the visual separation between your words and the quoted words in the indented block, no quotation marks are needed. An introductory lead-in prepares the reader for the long quotation, and a citation ends it.

Marking the boundaries of long quotations
- ◆ more than four lines
- ◆ one or more paragraphs

Boundaries are marked by a lead-in, a block indentation, and a citation.

Example 5.1.2.1

Paragraph, APA (indent five spaces or one-half inch):

Maheu and Gordon (2000) suggest that even as on-line technologies are being used increasingly for counseling and therapy purposes, these new modes of contact need to be assessed carefully:

> Each interactive technology raises new concerns related to its particular strengths and limitations. For instance, the use of videoconferencing involves both similar and different issues than does E-mail interaction with patients. Each technology needs to be examined separately for its related risk management issues. Likewise, each patient should be assessed for the need for and the suitability of on-line services, should be clearly informed of the nature and the limitations of the services, and should be given plans for possible equipment failures and crises. (p. 487)

Paragraph, MLA (indent ten spaces or one inch):

Marlene Maheu and Barry Gordon suggest that even as on-line technologies are being used increasingly for counseling and therapy purposes, these new modes of contact need to be assessed carefully:

> Each interactive technology raises new concerns related to its particular strengths and limitations. For instance, the use of videoconferencing involves both similar and different issues than does E-mail interaction with patients. Each technology needs to be examined separately for its related risk management issues. Likewise, each patient should be assessed for the need for and the suitability of on-line services, should be clearly informed of the nature and the limitations of the services, and should be given plans for possible equipment failures and crises. (487)

Comment:

Note that for both APA and MLA block quotation style, there are no quotation marks and the parenthetical citation floats after the final period. These are two differences from in-text quotations, where there are quotation marks and where the parenthetical citation is punctuated as part of the last sentence.

5.1.3 Marking the boundaries of an unquoted source.

When you rely on source material without quoting it, there are no quotation marks (or block indent), so the use of the introductory lead-in and a close (often a citation) is even more important because they alone function as the boundary markers. Your reader must be able to distinguish between your own ideas and arguments and those of the sources you use. Boundary markers are the only way to be clear about this.

Marking the boundaries of an unquoted source
- summarizing
- paraphrasing
- mentioning briefly
- using an idea from the source

Boundaries are marked by a lead-in and a citation or other close.

A paragraph that consists of a dozen or so lines of text with a citation only at the beginning or end is unfortunately common in students' research papers. In this type of paragraph, there is no indication how much of the paragraph draws upon the source mentioned in the citation. Does the citation apply to the whole paragraph or only the sentence containing the citation? Or does the writer intend it to apply to two or three sentences but not to all? Without both boundary markers, the citation alone can be confusing. Study the examples below to understand this problem more clearly and to learn how to remedy it.

Example 5.1.3.1

Source:

When a consumer product is subject to a recall order, it seldom travels anywhere. The order means that an identified fault must be remedied by the manufacturer. The remedy often involves only the mailing of new parts to the consumer or a visit to a repair center. —Jane Doe, 2000, p. 456

Hypothetical student paragraph with citation, APA style:

A product recall might be more accurately known as a product repair because most recalled products never leave the consumer's home. In many cases, when a defect is discovered by the manufacturer, a repair kit is sent to the consumer. In other cases, the product must be taken in for repair. Rarely will the product be called in and exchanged for another. For example, recalled automobiles are never returned to the factory and replaced; they are simply repaired at a dealer (Doe, 2000, p. 456).

Hypothetical student paragraph with citation, MLA style:

A product recall might be more accurately known as a product repair because most recalled products never leave the consumer's home. In many cases, when a defect is discovered by the manufacturer, a repair kit is sent to the consumer. In other cases, the product must be taken in for repair. Rarely will the product be called in and exchanged for another. For example, recalled automobiles are never returned to the factory and replaced; they are simply repaired at a dealer (Doe 456).

Comment:

In the paragraphs shown above, the student has not distinguished original ideas from a paraphrase of Doe. Neither an instructor nor any other reader will be able to tell how much of the paragraph is being attributed to the source. Note below the proper use of boundary markers.

Paragraph with boundary markers, APA style:

A product recall might be more accurately known as a product repair. As Doe (2000) notes, most recalled products never leave the consumer's home. In many cases, when a defect is discovered by the manufacturer, a repair kit is sent to the consumer. In other cases, the product must be taken in for repair. Rarely will the product be called in and exchanged for another (p. 456). For example, recalled automobiles are never returned to the factory and replaced; they are simply repaired at a dealer.

Paragraph with boundary markers, MLA style:

A product recall might be more accurately known as a product repair. As Jane Doe notes, most recalled products never leave the consumer's home. In many cases, when a defect is discovered by the manufacturer, a repair kit is sent to the consumer. In other cases, the product must be taken in for repair. Rarely will the product be called in and exchanged for another (456). For example, recalled automobiles are never returned to the factory and replaced; they are simply repaired at a dealer.

The use of both boundary markers in these two examples shows that the first part of the paragraph (renaming a recall to a repair) is the student's own idea, as is the example of the automobile recall at the end of the paragraph. Thus, including the proper boundary markers where they belong not only sets off the source but also clearly reveals the student's own ideas in the paragraph. As has been said before, *your own thinking is important*: It is a significant part of what your instructor expects. Give yourself credit, and be sure to show the difference between your ideas and those you are incorporating from research.

5.1.4 Marking the boundaries in problem cases.

Occasionally, situations arise when you must use a little creativity to construct your boundary markers. Example situations include these: (1) Web pages usually lack page numbers, (2) some Web pages show no author, and (3) citing an entire article or book in APA style does not require the use of page numbers. In these cases, there may be only one obvious item to use as a boundary marker.

One solution for indicating an end boundary is to show clearly that new material is beginning. One of the following markers may be appropriate:

- ◆ Start a new paragraph.
- ◆ Add a clear transition of thought (e.g., "Another researcher says").
- ◆ Show clearly that you are now commenting (e.g., "But Doe does not mention"; "Doe's implication is clear, for example, when").

Another solution is to use information about the source (author, title, subject, thesis, role in your paper) to create a second marker. The second marker serves to introduce the source and the citation information is moved to the end.

> **Example 5.1.4.1**
> Problem passage, entire article cited, APA style:
> Boolean logic frees the researcher from using only one keyword at a time. Doe (2002) says that using the appropriate forms of Boolean logic allows the searcher to control both the breadth of the search and the desired proximity of the search terms. This type of precision is simply impossible with paper indexes or printed bibliographies.
>
> Comment:
> This passage shows clearly that the first sentence belongs to the writer of the paper, while the second belongs to Doe. However, it fails to show that the last sentence belongs to the writer rather than Doe because there is no terminating boundary marker. In this case, the solution to the problem is to construct a second boundary marker by describing the author of the source, as in the following example:
>
> Improved passage, entire article cited, APA style:
> Boolean logic frees the researcher from using only one keyword at a time. A Library of Congress researcher says that using the appropriate forms of Boolean logic allows the searcher to control both the breadth of the search and the desired proximity of the search terms (Doe, 2002). This type of precision is simply impossible with paper indexes or printed bibliographies.

Example 5.1.4.2
Problem passage, Web page with no stated author or date, APA style:
According to "Making Lighting Work" (n.d.), when room lighting is designed, more than just lighting intensity (or brightness) needs to be taken into account. The color of the light and the location of the sources are also critical. Without consideration of all these factors, glare, eyestrain, and bizarre shadows can result.

Note: For APA, use "n.d." for *no date.*

Improved passage, Web page with no stated author or date, APA style:
According to an article on the Lighting Institute Web site, when room lighting is designed, more than just lighting intensity (or brightness) needs to be taken into account. The color of the light and the location of the sources are also critical. Without consideration of all these factors, glare, eyestrain, and bizarre shadows can result ("Making Lighting Work," n.d.).

Improved passage, Web page with no stated author or date, MLA style:
According to an article on the Lighting Institute Web site, when room lighting is designed, more than just lighting intensity (or brightness) needs to be taken into account. The color of the light and the location of the sources are also critical. Without consideration of all these factors, glare, eyestrain, and bizarre shadows can result ("Making Lighting Work").

Comment:
These improved passages neatly package the source material so that the writer is able to make comments before and after it in the same paragraph without creating any confusion in the reader's mind about whose ideas are being presented.

See Section 5.2 for more ideas for constructing boundary markers that are useful in problem cases.

5.1.5 Marking the boundaries for nontext information.

You will recall from Chapter 2 that all borrowed information must be cited, including photographs, drawings, tables, graphs, and so forth. The rules for citation are similar, taking into account the visual nature of the information.

Nontext information, such as a graph or table, sets itself off from your text by its visual form, much as a block indentation sets off a long, quoted text. Even so, this type of information includes boundary markers. For citation purposes, nontext information is divided into two categories, tables and figures. A table involves the presentation of words or data in a structured form. A figure includes a graph, a drawing, or a photograph.

In APA style, boundary markers for a table include a label at the beginning and a note with the citation at the end. If the table has been taken from a source exactly as it appears in the source, it is cited as *From,* but if you reorganize the data or take only part of it, the table is cited as *Adapted from.* (Note that for papers prepared for publication, a copyright notice naming the copyright holder of the source of the table is also included at the end of the bibliographic information, and if necessary a note that permission has been secured. See Example 5.1.5.3.)

Example 5.1.5.1
Table, APA style:

Table 3
Favorite Picnic Locations by Age

	>15	15-34	35-50	>50
Beach	52	31	25	22
Sunny Lawn	40	48	31	17
Shaded Tree	8	21	44	61

Note: Survey taken June 6, 2003. *n* = 346. From "Recreational Options As Influenced by Climate and Age," by J. Doe, 2003, *Journal of Leisure Time, 43*, p. 274.

In MLA style, table boundary markers are very similar to APA style, with the same beginning marker of the word *Table*, a number, and a title on the line below. The ending marker is similar also, with the word *Source* replacing the word *From*. The citation, of course, is in MLA style.

Example 5.1.5.2
Table citation, MLA style
Source: Jane Doe, "Recreational Options As Influenced by Climate and Age," *Journal of Leisure Time*, 43 (2003) 274.

For figures (graphs, drawings, and photographs) in APA citation style, the graphic itself provides the beginning marker (like a block indent), so you need only the ending marker, which consists of a label and a citation. The label should include the word *Figure* and a figure number and a title or caption for the figure. As with the table, if the graphic is pasted in exactly as it appears in the source, it is cited as *From*, but if you crop, enhance, or otherwise alter it, the graphic is cited as *Adapted from*. (As with a table, if your paper is being prepared for publication, include a copyright notice at the end of the bibliographic information.)

Example 5.1.5.3
Figure, APA style, with copyright and permission notice:

Figure 12. Creative thinking stimulus drawing. From *Creative Problem Solving* (p. 100), by R. A. Harris, 2002, Los Angeles: Pyrczak Publishing. Copyright 2002 by Pyrczak Publishing. Reprinted with permission.

Once again, for MLA style, boundary markers are similar to those in APA. The graphic provides its own beginning marker and the citation at the end follows MLA style. Note that MLA abbreviates the figure label to *Fig.* and does not italicize it.

Example 5.1.5.4
Figure citation, MLA style:

Fig. 12. Creative Thinking Stimulus Drawing. From Robert A. Harris, *Creative Problem Solving* (Los Angeles: Pyrczak, 2002) 100.

5.2 Introductory strategies.

As you may note from the examples in Section 5.1 above, part of the technique for marking the boundaries of a source involves an introductory lead-in of some kind. In addition to their role in honoring intellectual property and preventing plagiarism, introductory tags also help your reader understand how the source information fits into the argument of your paper.

5.2.1 Introduce your sources.

If you could be a fly on the wall of a coffeehouse, and if you could land near a table of instructors, you might hear the way they describe quotations that appear suddenly and without attribution in a paper: "disembodied quotations," "phantom words," "ghost quotations," "unannounced strangers." Rather than making a sudden and unexpected appearance, quotations should be introduced in some way that helps the reader prepare for them.

An introductory lead-in can include one or more of the following elements:

- **The author's name.**
    - According to Doe,
    - John Doe writes that
    - In an article by John Doe, we read
- **A description of the author** (credentials, job title, etc.).
    - A Yale University psychologist reports
    - A State of California geologist says
- **The title of the book or article.**
    - In *A History of Secret Codes*, we learn
    - The article, "The Botanical Source of Western Medicine," traces
- **The name of the journal or Web site.**
    - A study of the poet first appeared in *English Literary History*, discussing
    - The Procter and Gamble Web site offers information about
- **A brief summary of the content.**
    - In a discussion of the relationship between chocolate consumption and depression,
    - A rhetorical analysis of the poem has shown
    - A recent article about the design of room lighting tells us
- **An expression of the role of the quotation.**
    - Arguing exactly the opposite,
    - As evidence of this,
    - Coming to a similar conclusion by way of a different approach,
- **A combination of the above elements** (two or three at most).
    - Too many words, argues Jane Doe, can obscure meaning:

74

♦ John Doe, writing in the *Journal of the American Medical Association*, notes that many popular foods are high in fat:

♦ A report by a water analysis laboratory names the probable source:

5.2.2 Use a variety of introductory verbs.

"John Doe says" is always one way to introduce a quotation, of course. However, using the same introductory verb over and over will get old quickly. Choosing a variety of verbs will keep your writing from appearing mechanical. Another reason for using different verbs is that a carefully chosen one will help set up the quotation by giving your reader an indication of the role of the quotation. "John Doe shows" provides very different guidance from "John Doe objects."

The Table of Quotation Verbs on the following page offers a number of choices for you. The list is not exhaustive, but it will begin your thinking about the kinds of verbs you can use and the various ways you can prepare your reader for the role of the quotation in your paper.

5.2.3 Use introductory sentences with a colon.

Another strategy for introducing your sources is to include a sentence that presents helpful information to your reader about the nature or role of the quotation, followed by a colon. Here are some examples:

♦ Doe prefers an alternative approach:

♦ Doe reports that the source of the problem lies in a lack of early data:

♦ Doe distinguishes between the two:

♦ Doe reminds us of the idea's origin:

♦ Doe provides a possible solution to this problem:

♦ Doe argues that the evidence supports the earlier theory:

♦ Doe is careful to qualify the claims made by the Midland group:

♦ In support of this interpretation, Doe cites the change in temperature:

♦ After twenty-three years of research, Doe is ready to report the findings:

5.2.4 Use an introductory phrase.

Depending on the particular context of your source inclusion, you may want to use an introductory phrase rather than a verb. Here are some examples:

♦ In the words of Doe,

♦ According to John Doe,

♦ In Doe's view,

♦ As Doe tells us,

♦ As stated by John Doe,

♦ In the author's opinion,

When you use an introductory phrase, the quotation itself must be a complete sentence, or you must supply additional introductory words to make a complete sentence.

Table of Quotation Verbs

Says
The verb introduces the quotation as information.

    adds
    believes
    comments
    describes
    discusses
    emphasizes
    explains
    mentions
    notes
    observes
    offers
    points out
    remarks
    reports
    says
    states
    writes

Agrees
The verb indicates that the source agrees with another source or with the position you are advancing.

    accepts
    agrees
    assents
    concurs
    parallels
    supports

Yields
The source agrees that a conflicting point is valid.

    acknowledges
    admits
    agrees
    allows
    concedes
    grants
    recognizes

Argues in favor
The verb indicates that the source is providing evidence or reasons for a position.

    argues
    asserts
    contends
    demonstrates
    holds
    illustrates
    indicates
    insists
    maintains
    proposes
    shows

Argues against
The verb indicates that the source is responding critically to another source or with the position you are advancing.

    attacks
    contradicts
    criticizes
    denies
    differs
    disagrees
    disputes
    objects
    opposes
    rebuts
    refutes

States controversially
The source makes a statement that you are skeptical about (be careful of your tone if you use these).

    alleges
    assumes
    claims

Implies
The source presents information either tentatively or indirectly.

    implies
    proposes
    suggests

Continues
You continue to refer to or quote the source.

    adds
    continues
    goes on to say
    states further

Concludes
The source draws a conclusion from previous discussion.

    concludes
    decides
    determines
    finds

Example 5.2.4.1
Phrase introduction with quoted whole sentence, APA style:
According to Doe (1998), "The poet's personal letters were not discovered until 1915" (p. 567).

Phrase introduction with quoted whole sentence, MLA style:
According to Doe, "The poet's personal letters were not discovered until 1915" (567).

Example 5.2.4.2
Phrase introduction with quoted partial sentence, APA style:
In Doe's analysis (2004), the market for suntan lotion is "not entirely seasonal, but largely seasonal" (p. 345).

Phrase introduction with quoted partial sentence, MLA style:
In Doe's analysis, the market for suntan lotion is "not entirely seasonal, but largely seasonal" (345).

5.2.5 Use both set-off and built-in quotations.

A set-off quotation is presented to the reader in a formal way, with an introductory phrase, verb, or sentence, followed by a comma or colon. The quotation itself begins with a capital letter and usually consists of a complete sentence.

Example 5.2.5.1
Set-off with comma, APA style:
In a recent analysis of weather forecasting, Doe (2001) writes, "The accuracy of forecasts has increased remarkably as new technologies have become available" (p. 432).

Set-off with comma, MLA style:
In a recent analysis of weather forecasting, Jane Doe writes, "The accuracy of forecasts has increased remarkably as new technologies have become available" (432).

Example 5.2.5.2
Set-off with colon, APA style:
Doe (2000) is cautious about forecasts: "Never bet your umbrella on a forecast" (p. 234).

Set-off with colon, MLA style:
John Doe is cautious about forecasts: "Never bet your umbrella on a forecast" (234).

A built-in quotation places the quotation into a subordinate clause beginning with *that* and attaches the clause to the writer's sentence. There is no comma or initial capital letter:

Example 5.2.5.3
Built-in whole clause with *that*, APA style:
In a recent analysis of weather forecasting, Doe (2001) writes that "the accuracy of forecasts has increased remarkably as new technologies have become available" (p. 432).

Built-in whole clause with *that*, MLA style:
In a recent analysis of weather forecasting, Jane Doe writes that "the accuracy of forecasts has increased remarkably as new technologies have become available" (432).

Example 5.2.5.4
Built-in partial sentence with *that*, APA style:
In a recent analysis, Doe (2003) writes that the reliability of forecasts "has increased remarkably as new technologies have become available" (p. 432).

Built-in partial sentence with *that*, MLA style:
In a recent analysis, Jane Doe writes that the reliability of forecasts "has increased remarkably as new technologies have become available" (432).

See Section 5.3 below for more information and examples covering the variety of ways you can incorporate portions of sentences into your writing.

5.2.6 Use the historical present tense.

Students sometimes ask, "Because all of our sources were written in the past (even last week is now the past), shouldn't we be writing, 'John Doe *said*' instead of 'John Doe *says*'?" Other students ask a related question: "I can understand using *says* for a writer who is still alive, but what about a writer who has been dead for hundreds of years?"

The historical present tense is a convention (followed by many writers) that discusses and quotes all sources in the present tense. The historical present has the conceptual benefit of treating all ideas as equally alive and active, "in play," and available for consideration. As a practical benefit, the historical present helps your own writing to be more lively and interesting because you seem to be describing something happening right now rather than in the past. (Notice that the verbs in the Table of Quotation Verbs on page 76 are all present tense.)

Good advice, then, is to use the historical present tense for your papers where all of the ideas are still under active consideration. (This practice will also prevent your papers from falling into random tense shifting—changing back and forth unthinkingly between past and present tense—a common ailment in research-paper writing.) If you are comparing changes between the past and present or referring to ideas no longer active, it is acceptable to use the past tense. See Example 5.3.3.2 below.

5.3 Quoting strategies.

Quoting a complete sentence or two is only one way of bringing a writer's words into your paper. This section offers more ideas for incorporating quotations into your writing.

5.3.1 Interrupt quotations.

When you quote a complete sentence using a set-off introduction, you can do so according to Example 5.2.5.1 above, or you can divide the quotation into two pieces for the purpose of variety or emphasis.

Example 5.3.1.1
Divided quotation, APA style:
In a recent analysis, Doe (2001) notes the advances in the weather business. "The accuracy of forecasts has increased remarkably," she writes, "as new technologies have become available" (p. 432).

Divided quotation, MLA style:
In a recent analysis, Jane Doe notes the advances in the weather business. "The accuracy of forecasts has increased remarkably," she writes, "as new technologies have become available" (432).

Comment:
Note that the second piece of the sentence is a continuation of the first part, so that no capital letter is used. If you quote two separate sentences in this divided fashion, you will have a period ending the first sentence and a capital letter beginning the new, independent sentence, as in the following example.

Example 5.3.1.2
Two sentences, divided by comment, APA style:
Doe (2004) reminds us that a recalled product is often not sent anywhere: "The order means that an identified fault must be remedied by the manufacturer." In actual practice, she adds, "The remedy often involves only the mailing of new parts to the consumer or a visit to a repair center" (p. 456).

Two sentences, divided by comment, MLA style:
Jane Doe reminds us that a recalled product is often not sent anywhere: "The order means that an identified fault must be remedied by the manufacturer." In actual practice, she adds, "The remedy often involves only the mailing of new parts to the consumer or a visit to a repair center" (456).

5.3.2 Leave out some words.

An effective method of reducing a source's words while retaining the benefit of quoting exact words (rather than summarizing) is to leave out the words of lesser importance. (See Appendix A, Section A.4, for information about using ellipsis dots to show that words have been omitted from a quoted source.)

Example 5.3.2.1
Source:
Since its invention, the trend in video camera manufacture, like that of virtually all technology, has been toward the smaller, until we now have a camera that can be swallowed.
—John Doe, 2004, p. 132

Beginning omitted, APA style:
As Doe (2004) states, the development of the video camera "has been toward the smaller, until we now have a camera that can be swallowed" (p. 132).

Beginning omitted, MLA style:
As John Doe states, the development of the video camera "has been toward the smaller, until we now have a camera that can be swallowed" (132).

Middle omitted, APA style:
Technology researcher Doe (2004) indicates the direction of video design: "Since its invention, the trend in video camera manufacture . . . has been toward the smaller, until we now have a camera that can be swallowed" (p. 132).

Middle omitted, MLA style:
Technology researcher John Doe indicates the direction of video design: "Since its invention, the trend in video camera manufacture . . . has been toward the smaller, until we now have a camera that can be swallowed" (132).

Caution:
When you omit words from the middle of a sentence, be sure that the sentence still makes grammatical sense, and that you have not introduced an error such as a sentence fragment or comma splice. Also be sure that omitting the words does not change the meaning of the sentence.

End omitted, APA style:
Doe (2004) notes this trend toward miniaturization: "Since its invention, the trend in video camera manufacture, like that of virtually all technology, has been toward the smaller . . ." (p. 132).

End omitted, MLA style:
John Doe notes this trend toward miniaturization: "Since its invention, the direction in video camera manufacture, like that of virtually all technology, has been toward the smaller . . ." (132).

Comment:
Some instructors using MLA style prefer to have students put brackets around ellipsis dots that show the omission of words: "This is [. . .] sometimes preferred." Follow your instructor's requirements.

5.3.3 Quote phrases.

Often the most powerful quoting can be accomplished by using short phrases rather than entire sentences. By selecting just the phrase or phrases that best capture the idea you want to emphasize, you can build them into an appropriate sentence. Quoted phrases call attention to themselves because of their brevity and the highlighting effect produced by the quotation marks.

Example 5.3.3.1
Web article, no author, APA style:
The Tapwater Beverage Company promises that its new bottled water product will be manufactured using "state-of-the-art reverse osmosis filtration" that will guarantee "superiority of both purity and taste" ("Tapwater Enters," 2001).

Web article, no author, MLA style:
The Tapwater Beverage Company promises that its new bottled water product will be manufactured using "state-of-the-art reverse osmosis filtration" that will guarantee "superiority of both purity and taste" ("Tapwater Enters").

Comment:
In the example above, the name of the company that owns the Web site is used as the opening boundary marker and a shortened version of the title is used for the close. On the References page (for APA) or Works Cited page (for MLA), the article would be listed alphabetically by the first word of the title, and the entire title would be spelled out: "Tapwater Enters Bottled Water Business."

Using only the phrases that best contain the meaning of the sentence also allows you to adapt a sentence's tense, point of view, and other elements to produce agreement with your own writing. The following example clarifies this:

Example 5.3.3.2
Source:
We have no plans to expand into Asian markets at this time. —Jane Doe, 2003, p. 234

Tense and point of view change made, APA style:
In 2003, Doe announced that the company had "no plans to expand into Asian markets" at the time (p. 234). However, within a year, it was building distribution warehouses in three Asian countries.

Tense and point of view change made, MLA style:
In 2003, Jane Doe announced that the company had "no plans to expand into Asian markets" at the time (234). However, within a year, it was building distribution warehouses in three Asian countries.

Comment:
The source is an announcement made in the present tense, while the writer wants to use the past tense to recount past events. The announcement was also made in the first person plural (*we*) while the user of the source wants to use third person singular (*the company* and *it*). These changes are made outside the quotation. Then the quoted words are built into the sentence with the desired revisions.

Important Note: Remember that when you put words within quotation marks, you are promising your reader that those are the source's exact words. The rule for quotation, then, is this:

> **Always quote exactly.**

If words need to be changed, change words outside the quotation marks and quote only exact words. Use ellipsis dots to delete words within a quotation and square brackets to insert any words you are adding to make the meaning of the quotation clear. Never silently alter any quoted words. See Appendix A, Section A.4, for information and examples relating to the use of ellipsis dots and square brackets.

Review questions.

To see how well you understand this chapter, attempt to answer each of the following questions without referring to the text. (Write down your answers to make checking easier.) Then check your answers with the text. If you missed something important, add it to your answer.

1. In your own words, define the Simple Rule.

2. Why is it important to indicate the beginning and ending of the sources used?

3. Name several ways to introduce a source without naming the author.

4. What is the purpose of having different categories of introductory verbs?

5. Differentiate between a set-off and a built-in quotation.

6. What is the historical present tense and why is it used?

Questions for thought and discussion.

Use these questions for in-class discussion or for stimulating your own thinking.

1. What might be the result if your reader discovers that you have misquoted one of your sources?

2. Do you think that the process of using boundary markers will help you avoid unintentional plagiarism? Why or why not?

3. Explain how the skillful use of introductory tags and verbs can improve the logical coherence of your writing (that is, helping your reader understand where you are going and how the quotations fit into your discussion).

4. How does being able to quote pieces of sentences such as short phrases contribute to your writing effectiveness?

Name _____   Course _____

Chapter 5 Review: True-false quiz.

Directions: In each case, determine whether the statement is true or false.

1. A lead-in at the beginning and a citation (such as a page number) or other close form the boundary markers for a paraphrased source.
   ☐ True   ☐ False

2. If you don't have enough information about your source, such as a Web page with no author, you can omit the boundary markers.
   ☐ True   ☐ False

3. The boundary markers for a photograph taken from a source include a figure title and the bibliographic information from the source.
   ☐ True   ☐ False

4. If you alter the format of a table or figure, you must clearly indicate this change in your boundary marker by using the phrase *Adapted from*.
   ☐ True   ☐ False

5. When quoting a source from more than five years ago, you should use past-tense verbs, such as *said*, rather than present-tense verbs such as *says*.
   ☐ True   ☐ False

6. You should always quote complete sentences to offset the source's words from your own writing.
   ☐ True   ☐ False

7. It is permissible to make an unnoted change in a word or two in a source's sentence in order to make a quotation fit your sentence better grammatically.
   ☐ True   ☐ False

8. Long quotations are set off from the writer's text by a block indentation.
   ☐ True   ☐ False

9. A well-chosen introductory verb before a quotation can give your reader information about the purpose or intended effect of the quotation.
   ☐ True   ☐ False

10. Leaving words out of a source's sentence in a way that changes the meaning commits the fallacy of vicious abstraction even if you use ellipsis dots.
    ☐ True   ☐ False

Name _____   Course _____

Chapter 5 Review: Boundary markers.

Directions: For each example, decide whether or not the boundaries between the source use and the paper writer's own words have been adequately marked. In cases where the difference is not clear, suggest improvements. Finally, if the source is summarized or paraphrased, decide whether the use is properly constructed or commits plagiarism.

Source text.

Initially, oil rigs were required to be directly over the reservoir of oil they sought to pump out. Later, however, the development of slant drilling techniques permitted oil companies to reach multiple crude sources from a single drilling location, such as an offshore platform. Onshore, slant drilling allowed the exploitation of resources beneath developed areas. —John Doe, 1999, p. 123

Potential use 1, APA style.

In the early days of oil drilling, oil rigs were required to be directly over the reservoir of oil they sought to pump out. But then, as Doe (1999) writes, "the development of slant drilling techniques permitted oil companies to reach multiple crude sources from a single drilling location, such as an offshore platform" (p. 123). On land, slant drilling allowed the use of resources beneath developed areas.

Potential use 2, APA style.

Early oil rigs could drill only straight down, so that they had to be right on top of the pools of oil they tapped. Eventually, slant drilling enabled access to oil resources from locations far to the side of a given pool (Doe, 1999, p. 123).

Potential use 3, MLA style.

Oil drilling has not always been as flexible as it is today. In the early days, as oil historian John Doe tells us, drilling rigs had to be "directly over the reservoir of oil they sought to pump out" (123).

Potential use 4, MLA style.

In his discussion of the history of oil drilling, John Doe reminds us that the technique of slant drilling (drilling at an angle from a wellhead) was not available early on. Originally, the pool of oil to be tapped had to be directly under the wellhead. Only later could oil beneath settled land be tapped from the side, and multiple locations tapped from a single offshore rig (123).

Potential use 5, APA style.

Originally, writes Doe (1999), oil rigs had to be directly over the reservoir of oil they pumped. Later on, however, the invention of slant drilling procedures allowed oil companies to reach several oil sources from a single drilling spot, such as an offshore platform. On land, slant drilling permitted the drilling of oil beneath industrialized areas.

Notes

6
Effective Use

The power of quotation is as dreadful a weapon as any which the
human intellect can forge.
   —John Jay Chapman

Previous chapters have shown you how to select, prepare, and incorporate sources into your research-based writing. This final chapter takes you a step further by providing some practical techniques for making your source use particularly effective. In this chapter, you will learn some special techniques of source use.

♦ Introducing your sources more fully will give them greater credibility.

♦ Discussing the meaning or implications of the source clarifies its purpose and impact.

♦ Blending your sources into your writing will make your writing stronger.

♦ Avoiding the common pitfalls of ineffective source use will help you maintain your readers' confidence in your writing.

6.1 Introduce the source thoroughly.

Section 5.2 of the previous chapter discussed general strategies for introducing your sources. This section discusses several ways to add attention and credibility to the sources you use.

6.1.1 Establish the credibility of the source.

Going back at least to the time of ancient Greek and Roman oratory, speakers have traditionally been introduced, often by someone familiar to the audience, to attest to their trustworthiness. Ever since printed books have become available, prefaces and forewords by well-known people often recommend the books (and their authors) to the public. Your role as the introducer of a source is similar. When you say, "As John Doe says," your reader's first reaction might be to ask a few questions:

♦ Who is this John Doe?

♦ Why is he being quoted (or summarized or paraphrased)?

♦ Why should I believe him, anyway?

♦ What is this reference doing here?

In other words, your role as introducer of a source is to provide the reader with enough background that the source appears to be worthy of notice and even credit. You will recall that the first test of source evaluation, discussed in Chapter 3, Section 3.4.1, is *Expertise*. Now that you have located a source that has met the criteria for expertise, you may wish to offer some of the evidence of this expertise to your reader. Note the difference:

♦ As John Doe says, "These South American plants are dangerous."

♦ As John Doe, some guy with a Web page, says, "These South American plants are dangerous."

♦ As John Doe, author of *Poisonous Plants of South America*, says, "These South American plants are dangerous."

Clearly, the information provided in the last instance gives the reader much more reason to accept John Doe's comments as authoritative than does the information in the introductory language of the first two. The background information that helps build credibility of an author includes the following:

♦ organizational affiliation (e.g., of the Mayo Clinic)

♦ respected Web site (e.g., a government site: FDA, FTC, FBI, etc.)

♦ job description (e.g., coroner, geologist, forensic chemist, market analyst)

♦ relevant publications (e.g., name the cited or other publication)

♦ relevant accomplishments (e.g., war veteran, mountaineer, eyewitness)

Two words of caution are appropriate here. First, avoid making a bald authority appeal, which implies that a writer should be believed just because he or she possesses expert credentials or is associated with a famous organization. (See the fallacy of appeal to prestige in Chapter 3, Section 3.5.3.) The credentials tell us why we should listen to the source, but the quality of the source's arguments and evidence is what persuades us (or not) about the issue at hand. Second, use these introductions somewhat sparingly and keep them fairly brief, in order to keep the focus on the information under discussion rather than on the credentials.

Another way to establish credibility is to comment on the nature of the information itself, showing that the way it was acquired makes it likely to be dependable:

♦ In a major national survey, Doe (2003) has discovered that

♦ Based on interviews with seven eyewitnesses, Doe (2000) concludes

♦ An examination of the original autograph manuscript by Doe (2001) reveals

♦ After living with the tribe for two years, Doe (2004) writes that

♦ In an experiment with a more rigorous research model, Doe (2001) has corrected

The length of your credibility-establishing introduction depends on three factors:

♦ **How much of the source you use.** The amount of space you devote to a source, whether by quotation, summary, or paraphrase, indicates to some extent the degree of importance you place on it. The more you use of a source, then, the more space you should take to establish the source's credibility.

♦ **The nature of the source material.** If the source is presenting an uncontroversial historical narrative or providing some background information, a less elaborate introduction will be needed than if the source is providing analysis, expert opinion, evaluation, or judgment. Conclusions consisting of expert opinions or judgments require the presentation of credentials to give them weight and persuasive power.

♦ **How important the source is for your argument or discussion.** If you claim that the source provides substantial weight in favor of your position, you will need to establish credibility more thoroughly than if you bring in the source only as a minor support or as additional information.

As the examples above show, most credibility-building introductions should consist of just a few words. As a rule, even for sources with the most important impact in your paper, keep the maximum length of your introductory comments to less than ten words, and use such a length once or twice at most in a ten-page paper. Do not ramble on endlessly about how important or famous your source is.

6.1.2 Provide needed background or context.

In addition (or perhaps as an alternative) to providing information about the author, some information that puts the source material in context may be desirable. Explanation, history, contrasting ideas, the set-up of an experiment, or other information will often be useful for helping the reader understand the source.

> **Example 6.1.2.1**
> Historical background leads to quotation, APA style:
> Even a few years ago, individuals who prepared their own income taxes using tax software would have to wait until the "final version" of the software was released or make two trips to the computer store: one to get the preliminary version and a second to get the final version. With the advent of Web technology, however, that awkwardness has changed. As Doe (2002) notes, "Users can now buy the software anytime, knowing that an up-to-the-minute update is available twenty-four hours a day on the company's Web site" (pp. 61-62).

Pronounced impact can be created by describing a problem or question that the source then solves, answers, or at least discusses.

> **Example 6.1.2.2**
> Problem statement leads to quotation, MLA style:
> William Shakespeare had barely breathed his last before the controversy began over the authorship of the plays and other works attributed to him. Over the years, more than fifty candidates (including Queen Elizabeth) have been named, either individually or in groups, as writers of the works. The controversy has not been trivial, either: Mountains of tantalizing evidence have been brought together for each of the top half-dozen candidates (including Shakespeare himself). Renaissance scholar Jane Doe argues that the issue is not likely to be resolved anytime soon: "Each of the principal candidates such as Bacon and de Vere has too much circumstantial evidence to ignore and yet not enough to be finally convincing" (654).

6.1.3 Recommend the source.

In Chapter 5, you learned how helpful it can be to direct your reader's understanding of the role of a source by using appropriate introductory lead-ins, such as "Jane Doe agrees," or "Jane Doe has the opposite opinion." It can be equally useful and effective to recommend to the reader that particular attention to a source is desirable:

- Interestingly enough, John Doe reports that
- The most significant finding, however, comes from Jane Doe, who
- Doe identifies an important detail:
- The most insightful connection, however, is made by John Doe
- Indeed, as Doe suggests,

The word *indeed* is known as an expletive, a word used to emphasize a statement or part of a statement. Use of an expletive lets your reader know that the sentence is especially significant. Other expletives include *of course, to be sure,* and *clearly*.

Caution: Take care to be moderate in your recommendation. Avoid unprofessional or overly enthusiastic language, such as *amazing, incredible, wonderful, brilliant, absolutely convincing,* and the like.

6.2 Discuss or apply the source.

During the process of researching, thinking, and drafting, writers form many connections in their minds between the various materials being used. A quotation inserted to support a point may have a seemingly obvious link or purpose in the writer's mind. However, the reader has access only to the written words, not to the writer's thoughts. As a result, sometimes a reader is left wondering about the role of a quotation or other reference. An important task for you as a writer, then, is to be sure that the connections between elements are clear.

6.2.1 The purpose of a source is not always self-evident.

Sources (quotations, paraphrases, summaries, even brief references) do not explain themselves. Imagine your reader looking at the last source you inserted and asking one of these questions:

♦ What is this doing here?
♦ How does this reference apply to the point being discussed?
♦ How does this help advance the argument?
♦ What does this quotation mean?
♦ What should I especially notice in all these words?

As a thinking stimulus for yourself, imagine your reader reading over the quotation or paraphrase and saying, "Okay. I read that. I know what Doe says. So what?" Your task is to answer the "So what?" for your reader.

6.2.2 Explain the source.

The first way to help your reader understand the meaning and purpose of a quotation or other source use is to choose a good lead-in, as was discussed in Chapter 5, section 5.2. Instead of writing, "Doe says," use "Doe clarifies this," or "Doe offers a counter argument." After the use of the source, go on to explain or demonstrate how your lead-in is correct. Sources often need clarification, interpretation, commentary, or some other explanation. You may need to point out the significant detail or point if your use of the source is several lines long. As a rule of thumb, the more of a source you use, the longer your explanation should be. In fact, a good rule to follow is this:

Your explanation should be longer than the source material.

Some writers keep a loose scheme in their minds: The introductory lead-in should be from a fourth to half as long as the quotation, paraphrase, or summary; and the explanation following should be twice as long as the material being cited. Such a scheme may not fit every situation, but the general idea is interesting: The longer your source use, the more lead-in is desirable to build credibility or supply background, and the more explanation is needed to apply the source to the argument of the paper. The logic of this seems reasonable. The longer the use of the source, the more importance it takes on (why else are you using so much of it?), so there should be a lot to discuss. Imagine a six-line quotation with a one-sentence application following it: Your reader might think, "What's going on here?"

Just as the role of a source can be positioned for the reader by using an effective lead-in, so your comments can be positioned by a lead-in, also. Below is a table of interpretive lead-ins that will allow you to orient your reader's attention as you begin to explain the significance of your source.

Table of Interpretive Lead-Ins

What does it mean?
Here we see
From this we can understand
This means, in effect, that
In other words,

What does it not mean?
This does not mean, of course, that
No one would suggest from this that
This should not be understood to say

What does it imply?
With this comment Doe indicates
Doe appears to be implying here that
The implications of this fact are
The inference follows that
From this we can conclude that

What does it not imply?
It does not follow from this that
Here Doe does not appear to be implying
This fact still does not rule out
Yet it cannot be concluded that

Where does this lead?
As a result,
As a consequence,
This leads toward the conclusion that
This discovery greatly strengthens

How does this challenge or complicate?
Such a fact argues against the idea that
This, then, becomes a second hypothesis
Here, then, is still another complication

When you explain or interpret the source, do not restate or paraphrase it. If the quotation itself is unclear, you should probably paraphrase it *instead* of quoting it. If the quotation is clear, focus your commentary on applying it to your discussion. The point is to avoid saying the same thing the quotation says. Note in the following example how ineffective a redundant comment can be:

Example 6.2.2.1
Quotation with ineffective commentary, APA style:
In his analysis, Doe (2004) writes, "This bill for subsidizing buggy whip manufacture is ill-advised. It should be voted down" (p. 1414). Here, Doe says he is against the bill to subsidize buggy whip manufacture.

A better practice is to add a clarifying interpretation, the "So what?" that will help your reader understand the quotation.

> **Example 6.2.2.2**
> Quotation with improved commentary, MLA style:
> In his analysis, John Doe writes, "This bill for subsidizing buggy whip manufacture is ill-advised. It should be voted down" (1414). Doe realizes that subsidies for unneeded or marginal products represent a poor use of scarce public resources.

6.2.3 Be reasonable about the effect of the source.

Remember that an argument is built by offering multiple reasons and by appealing to evidence. No one piece will be overwhelming by itself even though it may be quite strong. Therefore, be careful not to attribute more convincing power to one source than it reasonably has. Rather than claim, for example, that a source *proves* a point or that it provides *overwhelming evidence*, you might say that it *lends weight* to the argument. Other reasonable claims include these:

- ♦ Doe's argument here presents a sturdy challenge to
- ♦ This seems to provide the best answer
- ♦ This is a credible argument that deserves serious consideration

The point of being modest is that making reasonable claims will increase your reader's confidence in your ability to evaluate and present evidence in a scholarly fashion.

6.2.4 Provide an example to clarify the source's point.

When a source treats an issue in general or abstract terms, you can aid your reader's understanding by supplying a clarifying example as part of your commentary. A concrete example creates an image in the reader's mind, making the concept more easily grasped.

> **Example 6.2.4.1**
> Summarized source followed by paper writer's examples, APA style:
> In his discussion of household electrical consumption, Doe (2001) argues that of the more than a dozen electrical motors in a typical home, the "occasional use" motors add significantly to the overall energy usage (pp. 246-252). Examples of occasional use motors would include bathroom vent fans, range hood fans, and garbage disposals because they are used only on occasion rather than continuously, as in the case of a refrigerator circulation fan.
>
> Comment:
> After the writer of the paper supplies several concrete examples, such as garbage disposals, the reader will have the knowledge of the term *occasional use motor* to follow the subsequent discussion with understanding.

> **Example 6.2.4.2**
> Quoted source followed by paper writer's examples, MLA style:
> A common style of literary criticism in the eighteenth century, writes John Doe, was to "point out the beauties and defects of a given work, with the idea that the critic would help build the public's taste as well as improve art itself" (321). Many issues of *The Tatler*

and *The Spectator* periodical papers by Joseph Addison and Richard Steele exemplify this practice.

6.3 Blend-in your sources.

Blending your sources into your writing can produce a particularly effective paper. By moving quickly back and forth from source to discussion, you show that you understand and can work with the source's ideas easily and fluidly.

6.3.1 Work your sources into the discussion.

Often, the centrally important core of information in a source can be found in just a phrase or portion of a sentence. In these cases, you can quote just that piece. If there are several such pieces, they can be assembled artfully into your discussion.

Example 6.3.1.1
Blended quotations, APA style:
During an investigation of the site, Doe (2004) found evidence of "early disturbances in most of the graves" (p. 233), with seven of them "plundered and virtually destroyed" (p. 254) by grave robbers. As a result of this activity, he concludes that the "entire site is largely compromised" (p. 221).

Example 6.3.1.2
Blended quotations, MLA style:
In her chapter on "The Power of Prepositions," Jane Doe notes that a small change in prepositions can produce "a dramatic alteration of the actual meaning" of a statement (453). For example, the expression "made of chicken" means that "the product is manufactured from chickens" (444), while the expression "made with chicken" may mean only that there was "one chicken among a thousand horses" (447).

6.3.2 Combine quoting with summarizing.

If quoting represents a regular-speed presentation of a source, summarizing represents fast-forward. By combining these two modes of use, you can regulate the tempo of the borrowing, speeding up and slowing down as the importance of the material warrants.

Example 6.3.2.1
Combined use, APA style:
In his article on Web search tools, Doe (2003) covers the general directories, such as Yahoo, containing the hand-picked sites of staff members or volunteers; the search engines, such as Google, indexing more than a billion pages of content; specialty search engines for subjects, such as law, medicine, and education; and search tools for the deep or invisible Web, which he finds "a rich and expansive realm of treasured content not often enough explored" by the average Web searcher (p. 365).

Example 6.3.2.2
Combined use, MLA style:
In his article on Web search tools, John Doe covers the general directories such as Yahoo, containing the hand-picked sites of staff members or volunteers; the search engines such as Google, indexing more than a billion pages of content; specialty search engines for subjects such as law, medicine, and education; and search tools for the deep or invisible

Web, which he finds "a rich and expansive realm of treasured content not often enough explored" by the average Web searcher (365).

6.3.3 Use *one long, many short* for powerful persuasion.

Especially in cases where you are building an argument, a successful strategy is to quote and discuss one source at some length to demonstrate its support, and then quote or refer to two or three other sources very briefly as additional examples of support. This practice offers the benefit of showing that several sources support your point, while saving you the time and space of detailing all of them.

Example 6.3.3.1

Long and short sources, APA style:

Advances in communication technology, argues Doe (2004), rather than enabling us to make better decisions, have deprived us of the ability to think. A hundred years ago, he says, a message required "three days by horseback or three months by ship" to go from one person to another, allowing for "substantial thinking time by both sender and receiver" between messages. Now, however, we are connected "instantly by fax, telephone, and Internet video," all of which demand instant, unthinking replies (pp. 464-465). Jones (2002) says much the same thing about our "thoughtless response time" (p. 114), as does Smith (2003).

Comment:

You may recall from Chapter 3, Section 3.4.3, that the credibility and reliability of information can be tested by seeking corroboration—the determination that the information is supported by more than one source. Specifically mentioned was triangulation, finding three sources that agree. Notice in the example just above that the writer has triangulated the sources for the reader: Three sources are cited that agree with each other. The corroboration has been accomplished briefly, yet it substantially strengthens the point the writer is making.

6.4 Avoid Ineffective Use.

Bringing in a source in an awkward or ineffective way can backfire on the writer of a paper by confusing or detouring the argument. When you use a source, then, take care to make the usage as strong as the rest of your paper.

6.4.1 Beware of long quotations.

Two crucial goals of your writing should be to keep your reader both interested in your discussion and focused on the central idea you are advancing. Lengthy quotations, and especially several lengthy quotations, tend to subvert both of these goals. No hard and fast rule about quotations exists, of course, and you can find many examples of books with half-page or even longer quotations as evidence that you may do the same. However, there are some good reasons to use great caution before using a quotation longer than about six or seven lines:

♦ **Long quotations look like padding** to many instructors (as was mentioned in Chapter 4, Section 4.2.2). If a long quotation is not discussed thoroughly (as recommended above in Section 6.2.2), it might appear even more arbitrarily inserted.

♦ **Many readers skip long quotations.** No quotation can be effective if it is not read. Readers closely following the discussion may think that they will lose their train of thought if they read a ten- or twenty-line quotation, so they may skim or even skip it altogether.

♦ **Readers may lose focus** when they do read through a long quotation (and then wish they had skipped it).

It is not uncommon for a long quotation to make only a single point that could be summed up or delivered in a short quotation taken from the longer one. Either form of condensing would make better use of your paper's space and your reader's time.

Example 6.4.1.1
Source, letter from a government authority regarding an urban legend:
We have investigated these claims thoroughly, subjecting them to our usual rigorous procedures for determining whether or not there is a factual basis behind them, and have concluded that the claims have no basis in fact. They remain unsubstantiated rumors spread persistently and yet without any discoverable merit. Parties wishing to contact the Agency for further information are welcome to do so. —John Doe, 2000

Comment:
One way to use this source would be to quote it in its entirety. However, you could make the same point (less boringly and, in fact, more powerfully) as follows:

Example 6.4.1.2
Abbreviated use, APA style:
In a letter on the Agency's Web site, Doe (2004), chief information officer, says that the Agency has "investigated these claims thoroughly" and that they have "no basis in fact."

If you seriously believe that your argument can best benefit by the quotation of more than forty or fifty words, your best approach will probably be to break the quotation up. Quote a portion and then discuss or apply that part; then quote some more. By breaking the quotation into several pieces, you will not only better maintain your voice in the paper but also more clearly preserve the flow of the argument or discussion. You also show more clearly what parts of the source you are addressing in your comments.

6.4.2 Avoid overuse of one source.

Whether or not you have a minimum number of sources you must include in your paper, be careful not to rely excessively on a single source. Overuse can take several forms:

♦ **Citing the same source several times in a row.** Using a source several times by following the same order of presentation as the source (such as pages 234, 255, 276, or worse, pages 234, 235, 237) creates the appearance that the source is merely being summarized and transferred into the paper without any further processing, analysis, or integration into the overall argument. A better practice is to collect all your sources and arrange them in the most useful order before you begin drafting.

♦ **Citing a source sequentially.** Even when other sources are placed between sequential uses of a single source, the effect is much the same as that just described:

The writer appears to be copying without thinking rather than constructing a purposefully organized discussion.

♦ **Citing a source too many times.** Regardless of the order or location of multiple uses of a single source, relying on a single source more than just a few times usually implies inadequate research and thinking.

When you write a paper of any kind, even a book review, take command of the organization of ideas and the structure of the presentation. Put the concepts and your comments into the arrangement you believe to be the most effective. Readers expect reviewers to engage the material and present it in a clear way, and many instructors are wary of reviews that follow exactly the order of ideas in the book: They know all too well that some students type a bit, turn a few pages, type a bit more, turn a few more pages, and so on, the night before the paper is due.

6.4.3 Begin and end each paragraph with your own words.

Usually it is best to avoid beginning a paragraph with the use of a source (quotation, paraphrase, or summary) because that leaves no room to set up the topic of the paragraph and introduce the source. Similarly, unless a quotation is used for effect (such as a proverb or provocative statement), it is usually best to end the paragraph by applying the quotation and then concluding the paragraph with your own further discussion. The same policy holds true for summaries and paraphrases.

6.4.4 Be sure citations match the references.

Experienced instructors know that this piece of obvious advice bears reinforcing. The purpose of an in-text citation (both APA and MLA) is to allow the reader to find the full bibliographic entry among the References (APA) or Works Cited (MLA) at the end of the paper. Simply put, if the citation says "Doe (2003)," there should be an entry in the bibliography under "Doe" as the first word of the entry. If an article or other source is anonymous and the citation uses a short title, such as "Tea Trade," there should be an entry under "Tea Trade" as the first words. This cross-referencing from in-text citation to bibliography is also why the entries in the bibliography are alphabetized: to permit easy location of the cited works.

To avoid creating the impression of being an unskilled writer, you should be sure that every citation has an exactly matching entry in the bibliography, which is carefully alphabetized. You will also thereby avoid being suspected of faking a citation. Citation faking is a serious act of academic dishonesty, often found in connection with plagiarism and punished similarly. Take care to avoid any suspicion of this dishonest practice.

Review questions.

Directions: To see how well you understand this chapter, attempt to answer each of the following questions without referring to the text. (Write down your answers to make checking easier.) Then check your answers with the text. If you missed something important, add it to your answer.

1. What is the purpose of introducing a source?

2. Why is it important to establish the credibility of a source you quote?

3. What is the function of an *interpretive lead-in*?

4. Explain the concept of finding multiple sources that agree as an indicator of source credibility.

Questions for thought and discussion.
Use these questions for in-class discussion or for stimulating your own thinking.

1. When you read a book or article that makes substantial use of sources, what are some of the things that help you decide how much importance or plausibility you give to each source?

2. Which techniques in this chapter do you think will help improve the persuasiveness of your own writing with sources, and why?

3. What are some places you might find background information or context to help set up a quotation from a source?

4. In what ways are you responsible to your reader and to your source when you use a source in a research paper?

Name _____   Course _____

Chapter 6 Review: True-false quiz.

Directions: In each case, determine whether the statement is true or false.

1. To avoid the fallacy of the appeal to prestige, you should not mention a source writer's personal title, job title, or organizational affiliation.
   ☐ True   ☐ False

2. The more of a source you use, the more robust your introductory information should be for that source.
   ☐ True   ☐ False

3. You should **not** make up your own examples to clarify a source's discussion. Use only the examples mentioned by the source.
   ☐ True   ☐ False

4. If you quote or otherwise draw on a source at length, your explanation and application of the source's purpose and role in your argument should usually be proportionately lengthy.
   ☐ True   ☐ False

5. Clarifying what a source does **not** mean is sometimes an effective interpretive strategy.
   ☐ True   ☐ False

6. Your reader's confidence in your argument is likely to be increased if you make moderate rather than dramatic claims about the persuasiveness of a source.
   ☐ True   ☐ False

7. Quoting and summarizing should **not** be combined because the result will be plagiarism.
   ☐ True   ☐ False

8. Using several sources that agree with each other should be avoided in order to prevent redundancy. Use no more than two sources that make the same point.
   ☐ True   ☐ False

9. Lengthy quotations sometimes cause readers to lose their focus on the central idea of the paper.
   ☐ True   ☐ False

10. By making sure that every citation in the body of your paper has an exactly matching entry in the bibliography (References or Works Cited), you can help avoid being suspected of citation faking.
    ☐ True   ☐ False

Name _____   Course _____

Chapter 6 Review: Effectiveness.

Directions: For each paragraph below, comment on what makes the passage ineffective and say how it can be improved. (Note: This exercise uses APA citation style.)

1. The telecommunications industry is in turmoil. "The Internet is threatening to make long-distance phone calling free, for example" (Doe, 2003, p. 144). Also, the world may soon go wireless.

2. In an article on natural hair care, Doe (2002) reveals that most commercial shampoos are very damaging to hair. This proves that natural hair cleansers are better for you than commercial shampoos.

3. Doe (2000) says, "Clay soils need amendments to provide a loosening effect" (p. 234). Doe (2000) adds, "Water does not penetrate clay soils well" (p. 235). Another thing Doe says is, "Sand, therefore, can serve as a useful additive for soils of low permeability like clay" (p. 237).

4. Doe (2004) reports that credible information about various Internet hoaxes is available by "consulting the Hoaxbusters Home Page, which is operated by the CIAC" (p. 144).

5. According to the United States Department of State (2000), travel warnings are issued when it is dangerous to travel in a country: "Travel Warnings are issued when the State Department decides, based on all relevant information, to recommend that Americans avoid travel to a certain country. Countries where avoidance of travel is recommended will have Travel Warnings as well as Consular Information Sheets" ("Travel Warnings").

6. In spite of government reassurances, however, Doe (2003) provides a devastating counterargument, revealing that there are no guarantees of safety with this product: "You could be killed if you use it" (p. 333).

7. Increased noise can be a byproduct of economizing. According to Doe (2002), "The refrigeration compressor became noisier as a result of increasing its speed by reducing the amount of internal windings in order to save manufacturing costs. Ventilation air noise increased as higher speed fans (noisier in themselves) were used to push more air through smaller, and hence cheaper, ducts, which then rattled from the air velocity. Less expensive mounting techniques produced whole room vibrations, hums, and even thumps as equipment cycled on and off. We therefore experience today a whole symphony of noise created by the desire to cut costs" (pp. 234-235).

Notes

Appendix A
Polishing Your Prose

This appendix contains a series of tips and exercises to help you improve the polish and accuracy of your writing. Each of these items represents an area of grammar, mechanics, or punctuation that writers of research papers often miss. The tips will help remedy the most common error patterns encountered in student writing. Master these points and you will improve the technical quality of your research paper substantially.

A.1 Beware of thesaurusitis.

The purpose of writing is to communicate, not to obscure your ideas by showing off an abstract vocabulary. A good vocabulary is important for the clearest expression, but choosing words merely for the sake of impressing the reader is a mistake. Words should be chosen for their accuracy and appropriateness to the context.

Thesaurusitis is a condition that often seizes young writers who wish to impress their readers. These writers use a thesaurus to look up many of the words they have written and then substitute the longest words they can find. Unknown to them, the result is not a seemingly sophisticated paper that impresses their instructor. Rather, the result is often quite comical, causing any educated reader to laugh at it. There are several reasons for the failure of thoughtless substitutions to be effective.

- **There are several levels of language use.** For example, a competent writer would not mix slang words with formal words like this: "Your honor, this bad dude has committed a serious violation of the traffic code." Similarly, some words are more fitting in a formal or an informal context. The thesaurus does not label which level of diction (language use) each word belongs to, and sometimes the usage practice is rather subtle. To put it another way, words cannot be mixed together without consideration of their usage level.

- **Synonyms often have only similar meanings.** The thesaurus contains synonyms, but a synonym often does not mean exactly the same thing as another word. More commonly, *a synonym means something similar to another word*. The similarity varies. You may have seen some of the comical results from using synonyms. Here is an example, constructed by using a synonym dictionary, showing that *love* means *hatred* because they are synonyms:

> Love is synonymous with Affection.
> Affection is synonymous with Concern.
> Concern is synonymous with Carefulness.
> Carefulness is synonymous with Exactness.
> Exactness is synonymous with Strictness.
> Strictness is synonymous with Criticism.
> Criticism is synonymous with Disapproval.
> Disapproval is synonymous with Aversion.
> Aversion is synonymous with Hatred.

♦ **Words are often used in ways that do not transfer to synonyms.** Figurative use of words and ideas, idioms, and even clichés affect the interpretation of words and phrases, changing their meaning from a literal understanding to something more nuanced. Suppose a student writes in a paper, "Last night my roommate was dead wrong about when the bookstore closed." Wanting to impress the instructor, the student looks up two words in the thesaurus and substitutes them this way: "Last night my roommate was deceased unlawful about when the bookstore closed." Clearly, *deceased* and *unlawful*, though synonyms for *dead* and *wrong*, respectively, cannot be thoughtlessly substituted for those words in just any situation. And yet, the resulting sentence is not much different from the writing many instructors receive.

Build your vocabulary as you read and study because the more words you know, the more exact you can be in your thinking and writing. Words should add clarity to ideas as you write, not muddy them. Do not use big words for their own sake; in other words (using the thesaurus), eschew the gratuitous utilization of sesquipedalian locutions. For the best writing, then, learn a lot of useful words and follow this advice:

When you write, use the words you know.

Exercise A.1: Synonyms.

Look up the word *clear* in a thesaurus (synonym dictionary) and choose any five synonyms listed. Next, using a regular dictionary, look up each of the five words and write out their definitions.

What can you conclude about the nature of synonyms and thesauruses?

A.2 Punctuation.

When you use a source that follows British rather than American conventions for quotation (such as using single rather than double quotation marks), you should convert the punctuation use to American conventions while leaving the spelling and grammar of the original unchanged. The reason for this is that punctuation is traditionally considered a printer's convention, and every document should be consistent in its conventions.

Research papers that mix conventions (sometimes putting commas inside quotation marks, sometimes outside, for example) appear to be careless and unprofessional, as if the writer had not performed even basic proofreading. Consistency is a type of accuracy, and accuracy—or its absence—sends a message about the writer's competence to the reader.

On the next page is a summary of the most common American conventions for punctuating quotations.

Quotation Rule	Example
1. Quotations use double quotation marks.	"Follow American conventions," he says.
2. Periods and commas go inside quotation marks.	The instructor says, "Remember where the comma goes," and adds, "and periods, too."
3. Quoting within a quotation uses single quotation marks.	The waiter said, "Our cake has been called 'chocolate decadence' by the food critics."
4. Quoting one word uses double quotation marks. The punctuation goes inside.	She called the spa "rejuvenating" and "fun."
5. A parenthetical citation is part of the sentence but not part of the quotation.	APA: The book says, "Try this" (p. 123). MLA: The book says, "Try this" (123).

Rule 2 above is perhaps the most commonly broken in student writing. Unless you have a citation that moves the period after the parentheses (see Rule 5), periods and commas go inside the quotation mark.

Rule 4 emphasizes quoting a single word as a quotation from a source. Be sparing in your use of quotation marks to call attention to your use of a word, with the implication that you disagree with the appropriateness of the use. Such a practice is known as using *scare quotes* or *sneer quotes* because the quoter seems to be sneering at the source's use of the words. Further, take care to avoid putting any of your own words in sneer quotes, as if you disavow the words themselves. As you can see, such a "habit" is usually seen as a sign of "immaturity," and is not an "effective" writing practice.

Exercise A.2: Punctuation.

Directions: Each of the following sentences contains errors in the use of punctuation and quotation marks. Rewrite each sentence to correct the errors.

1. Jane noticed that the leaves at the top had "yellow splotches", "green stripes", and "black spots" on them.

2. Be sure to print using 'photoenhanced ink' for the best results.

3. APA: Doe (2003) writes, "This study required three years to conduct (p. 123)."
   MLA: John Doe writes, "This study required three years to conduct (123)."

4. The experimenter's notes often used the word "protracted".

5. The speaker asked, "What is this "cornucopia of life" you mentioned?"

A.3 Spelling and Grammar.

Because your readers cannot see you, they take cues about who you are—how smart, how believable, how well educated, how knowledgeable—from the way you write, and particularly from how accurate you are. For this reason, *accuracy is crucial.*

Check your spelling.

The most obvious indicator of accuracy is spelling. The simple fact is that readers do not trust writers who cannot spell. The most glaring of spelling errors is that of authors' names or the titles of works. Spelling these items correctly is simply a matter of copying. Writers who cannot copy accurately are often viewed as either careless, ignorant, or incompetent, and therefore unworthy of reading. If you wish your writing to be read with credibility, be extra careful about accuracy. Double-check the names, the bibliography, the titles.

The other energetically waving red flag that puts readers off is the spelling of the same word in several different ways. Even readers who may forgive misspelling a word wrong repeatedly (the same way each time) are likely to be put off completely if they see the same word in three or four different spellings.

Watch your grammar.

An excellent way to brush up your grammar skills is to look over a grammar review or composition book for ten or fifteen minutes a day until you cover all the areas about which you are still unclear. Many of these books contain sections that focus on the most common errors, and a look at those items might prove beneficial.

To give you a start, here are three of the most common grammar errors found in student writing.

Comma splice. A comma splice (sometimes called a comma fault) occurs when two complete sentences are connected to each other using only a comma.

> Example comma splices:
> The leaves had a wax-like coating, the stems had thorns.
>
> The sandy area eroded rapidly, however, the rocky hill showed little change.
>
> A photograph of the footprint was presented as evidence, later, a plaster cast was introduced as well.
>
> The correlation between the two factors was not statistically significant, thus, there was probably not a cause-effect relationship.

As several of the examples above show, a comma splice often occurs when the writer mistakenly believes that an adverb (such as *later, thus, however, then*) can function as a conjunction to join the two sentences with a comma.

Comma splices can be corrected in any of several ways. Here are some examples:

Comma splice corrected with a period:
The leaves had a wax coating. The stems had thorns.

Comma splice corrected with a semicolon:
The sandy area eroded rapidly; however, the rocky hill showed little change.

Comma splice corrected with a coordinating conjunction:
A photograph of the footprint was presented as evidence, and later, a plaster cast was introduced as well.

Comma splice corrected by subordinating one of the clauses:
Because the correlation between the two factors was not statistically significant, there was probably not a cause-effect relationship.

Note that the one way a comma splice cannot be corrected is simply to delete the comma. Such an act creates a fused sentence.

Comma splice turned into a fused sentence:
The leaves had a wax coating the stems had thorns.

Fused sentence. A fused (or run-together) sentence occurs when two complete sentences are written without an indication of where one sentence ends and the other begins.

Examples of fused sentences:
The paper fed from the tray the printer began to squeak.

The original telescopic image is in black and white the computer adds the color.

Fused sentences can be corrected in any of the same ways as comma splices.

Fused sentence corrected by subordinating one of the clauses:
After the paper fed from the tray, the printer began to squeak.

Fused sentence corrected by adding a semicolon:
The original telescopic image is in black and white; the computer adds the color.

Sentence fragment. A fragment is a piece of a sentence (in other words, an incomplete sentence) punctuated as if it were a whole sentence. Some writers use fragments intentionally, for special effect, but often in student work the fragments are unintentional and awkward. In some cases, the fragment belongs to the sentence next to it.

Example fragments that belong to adjacent sentences:
Minerals are added to improve taste. After the water is purified.

105

Most photo editing software provides saturation control. To improve color intensity.

Sentence fragments are corrected either by changing the fragment into a complete sentence or by attaching the fragment to the sentence to which it belongs.

> Fragment corrected by being changed into a sentence:
> Minerals are added to improve taste. This step occurs only after the water is purified.

> Fragment corrected by attaching it to the sentence to which it belongs:
> Most photo editing software provides saturation control to improve color intensity.

Exercise A.3: Grammar.

In each case, identify the error as a comma splice, fused sentence, or fragment. Then rewrite the sentence, correcting the error.

1. Some early maps of the world were intended to be symbolic they were not used for navigation.

2. The risk of cancer from this chemical is now in doubt. Although the issue remains controversial.

3. We should ask whether the sample was truly random, then we could better judge how much confidence to put in the results.

A.4 Ellipsis and Square Brackets.

Words cannot be omitted or added to a quotation unless you inform your reader. Use ellipsis dots to show where you have omitted words, and use brackets to show where you have inserted words.

Ellipsis.

Ellipsis dots consist of three periods with spaces between them. They are used to indicate the omission of words from the middle or at the end of a quotation (but not the beginning). With publication of the most recent versions of the *Publication Manual of the American Psychological Association* (5th ed., APA, 2001) and the *MLA Handbook for Writers of Research Papers* (6th ed., Gibaldi, 2003) ellipsis dots are treated the same. However, the *MLA Handbook* notes that some instructors prefer to enclose ellipsis dots with brackets to show that they have been inserted by the writer of the research paper rather than by the original author. Follow your own instructor's preference.

Example source:
Do not tie your shoe in a melon patch or adjust your hat under a pear tree. —Chinese Proverb

Example use 1:
APA: A Chinese proverb reminds us to avoid actions that casual observers may misinterpret: "Do not . . . adjust your hat under a pear tree."
MLA: A Chinese proverb reminds us to avoid actions that casual observers may misinterpret: "Do not . . . adjust your hat under a pear tree."
Optional MLA: A Chinese proverb reminds us to avoid actions that casual observers may misinterpret: "Do not [. . .] adjust your hat under a pear tree."

Comment:
Words omitted from the middle of the quotation are indicated by three spaced periods.

Example use 2:
APA: The Chinese proverb says, "Do not tie your shoe in a melon patch. . . ."
MLA: The Chinese proverb says, "Do not tie your shoe in a melon patch. . . ."
Optional MLA: The Chinese proverb says, "Do not tie your shoe in a melon patch [. . .]."

Comment:
When the ellipsis is at the end of the sentence, there is a fourth dot, which is the period ending the sentence. The period follows the last letter, except for the optional MLA style.

Example use 3:
APA: We should be careful to avoid suspicious behavior: "Do not tie your shoe in a melon patch . . ." (Chinese proverb).
MLA: We should be careful to avoid suspicious behavior: "Do not tie your shoe in a melon patch . . ." (Chinese proverb).
Optional MLA: We should be careful to avoid suspicious behavior: "Do not tie your shoe in a melon patch [. . .]" (Chinese proverb).

Comment:
If there is a citation at the end, the period moves from after the last letter of the quotation to after the end of the citation.

Example use 4:
APA: A Chinese proverb says not to "tie your shoe in a melon patch. . . ."
MLA: A Chinese proverb says not to "tie your shoe in a melon patch. . . ."

Comment:
The omission of words from the beginning of a quotation does not need to be signaled because the quotation is clearly beginning mid-sentence or begins with a lower-case letter. The omission at the end needs to be indicated to let the reader know that more words follow in the original source.

Square brackets.

Square brackets are used to add words into the middle of a quotation. Parentheses are not used because then readers might think the original source had used the parentheses, and confusion would result. Inserting words may be desirable under several circumstances.

◆ **To clarify a pronoun by adding the word to which it refers.** The reference word (called the antecedent) may be in a previous sentence not included in the quotation. Example: "Fresh gouges were clearly visible where it [the rim of the wheel] contacted the pavement."

◆ **To add clarity or explanation.** Example: "The sampling records [from the mountain weather stations] were examined for levels of the same atmospheric gasses."

◆ **To identify an obvious error in the source text**, so that it will not appear to be a copying mistake. The Latin word *sic* (meaning *thus*) is used. The word is underlined or italicized in APA style but not in MLA style. APA example: "The general's words, however, should be understood in the contrext [*sic*] of the surrounding battle." MLA example: "He despised valed [sic] threats."

Exercise A.4: Ellipsis.

Rewrite each of the following sentences, leaving out the underlined words and inserting the appropriate ellipsis dots.

1. As Doe (2003) reminds us, "The patient experiences only the interaction with the nurses, not their total knowledge or ability <u>garnered from her educational training or years of experience</u>" (p. 416).

2. Doe's conclusions are "based on a careful examination <u>(made possible by the library)</u> of archival documents originating at or near the time of the battle itself" (213).

A.5 Style.

Your instructor may have told you that research papers should be written in a formal style. A useful definition of formal style might be "writing on its best behavior." Writing is expected to be more accurate and more careful than everyday speech. For example, formal writing avoids slang and colloquial expressions ("this idea is totally hot"), vagueness ("different people have different ideas"), and incorrect grammar ("everyone loses their rights"). Additionally, several commonly used expressions create not only an informal but also an unprofessional feel to a paper. For more effective writing, take care to avoid these:

◆ In this quotation, it says [use the writer's name, as in *Here, John Doe says*]
◆ The author is trying to say [use *the author says* or *Doe says*]
◆ In today's society [say *today* or *now*]
◆ This proves [*proves* is usually too strong; try *shows, argues,* or *indicates*]
◆ This article talks about [too informal; try *John Doe discusses*]
◆ In this quote, he says [*quote* is a verb, not a noun: use *quotation*]
◆ This is a common ad [spell words out fully: *advertisement* here]
◆ We don't know the effects yet [avoid contractions: use *do not* here]

♦ And this, I feel, is important [say simply that *this is important*]
♦ I may be wrong about this, but [avoid apologizing for your ideas]

Exercise A.5: Style.

Directions: Rewrite each of the following sentences, improving the effectiveness by revising the underlined awkward and informal expressions.

1. In "Overeating Aversion Training," the article talks about giving mild electric shocks to laboratory rats to keep them away from the food trough.

2. Jane Doe is trying to say that negative stimuli can be effective, which, I feel, is an important point.

3. In her quote given above, it says that we have fewer disincentives to overeat in today's society.

A.6 Pronouns.

Pronouns are parts of speech that refer to nouns. Pronouns include *you, we, it,* and *they*. Incorrect use of pronouns creates numerous errors in student writing.

Pronoun agreement.

When you use a pronoun, it must agree in number (singular or plural) with the noun to which it refers. A frequent error made by student writers is to use a plural pronoun to refer to a singular noun. To produce a grammatical construction, the noun and the pronoun must be either both singular or both plural. Note the following errors and their corrections:

> Original with error:
> The company announced higher earnings. They will be increasing their dividend.

> Improved versions:
> The company announced higher earnings. It will be increasing its dividend.
> The company executives announced higher earnings. They will be increasing the dividend.

> Original with error:
> We asked the committee for a delay, but they said no.

> Improved versions:
> We asked the committee for a delay, but it said no.
> We asked the members of the committee for a delay, but they said no.

Pronoun reference.

Another frequent error is the use of a pronoun without any noun to which it can refer. An isolated *it* or *they* makes writing unclear because your reader must guess about the thing or person you intend. Be careful, then, to supply a noun referent for each pronoun you use. Note the following ungrammatical uses and their corrections:

Original with error:
In this advertisement, they claim that the product will remove wrinkles.

Improved version:
This advertisement claims that the product will remove wrinkles.

Original with error:
A study was made about the effects of salty soil on crop yield. They found that salty soil had varying effects.

Improved versions:
A study was made about the effects of salty soil on crop yield. Researchers found that salty soil had varying effects.

Researchers studied the effects of salty soil on crop yield. They found that salty soil had varying effects.

Indefinite pronouns.

Indefinite pronouns form a category of pronouns. They include *anyone, anybody, someone, somebody, everyone, everybody, one,* and *person*. Indefinite pronouns are all singular and therefore must be referred to by another singular pronoun. Note these errors and their corrections:

Original with error:
Everyone must make their own judgment about this.

Improved versions:
Everyone must make his or her own judgment about this.
Everyone must make a personal judgment about this.

Original with error:
A person should consider their ability to accept risk before investing.

Improved versions:
A person should consider his or her ability to accept risk before investing.
People should consider their ability to accept risk before investing.

The grammatical remedy of using "his or her" to agree with an indefinite pronoun is not very elegant, especially if used frequently. A better solution is to use fewer indefinite pronouns. Computer analysis of student and professional writing reveals that student writers use indefinite pronouns ten times more often than professionals do. The result can be writing cluttered with "he or she" and "his or her." To use fewer indefinite pronouns, substitute plural nouns relevant to the context. Note these examples:

Acceptable but awkward:
When someone uses an industrial dishwasher, he or she must be careful not to be scalded.

Improved version:
Operators of industrial dishwashers must be careful not to be scalded.

Acceptable but awkward:
A person should always take his or her coat to a night baseball game.

Improved version:
Baseball fans should always take their coats to a night game.

Acceptable but awkward:
Everyone should write his or her name on the test booklet.

Improved version:
Test takers should write their names on the test booklet.

Avoid the ambiguous *you.*

A final, common problem with pronouns is the use of *you* to refer to no one in particular. For example, "When you pet your dog, you can see his tail wag." In a situation like this, your reader may very well reply, "What are you talking about? I don't even have a dog." Use *you* only to refer directly and specifically to your reader, not as a substitute for *someone.* Note also that the use of *you* and *I* are appropriate at relatively informal levels of writing; most academic papers are intended to be written at a more formal level.

Exercise A.6: Pronouns.

Directions: Each of the following sentences contains an incorrect or ineffective use of a pronoun. Rewrite each sentence, correcting the error or improving the effectiveness.

1. The organization has not yet released a statement, but they should do so soon.

2. Some hoaxes are very believable. When you first hear them, you are deceived by the details, even though you realize later that the details cannot be checked.

3. A report was issued regarding the cause of the accident, in which they said it was weather related.

111

4. The theft of the Web site's database means that anyone who purchased an item from the site has had their credit card information stolen.

5. If you need more tax forms, visit the local post office. They have a good supply.

Appendix B
Citation Examples

Both the Modern Language Association and the American Psychological Association publish entire books dealing with citation issues to help research paper writers. There are many varieties of books (single author, multiple author, editor, series, editions, and so on) and articles, as well as other kinds of information sources (the Web, electronic databases, charts, recordings). In a brief space here, only the most common bibliographic examples can be given. For more information, consult one of the official publications or a grammar handbook.

APA style: References.

Typical book.
Last name, Initial(s). (Year). *Book title: Subtitle.* City of Publication: Publisher.

Doe, J. S. (2004). *Interrupted speech: Communication by intrusion.* London: Social Behavior Press.

Typical article.
Last name, Initial(s). (Year). Article title. *Periodical Title, Volume,* Pages.

Doe, J. (2002). Computer simulation of laboratory rat behavior. *Journal of Computer Simulation, 18,* 112-122.

Typical Web page.
Last name, Initial(s). (Year). *Document title.* Retrieved date, from Web site: URL

Doe, J. P. (2003). *Survey of freshmen attitudes towards work-study.* Retrieved October 15, 2003 from Tustin Metropolitan University, Department of Psychology Web site: http://www.tmu.edu/psych/frosh.html

Typical database.
Last name, Initial(s). (Year). Article title. *Periodical Title, Volume,* Pages. Retrieved date, from database.

Doe, J. (2002). Advertising and the demand curve. *Journal of Media Practices, 54,* 344-365. Retrieved January 14, 2004 from Ebsco Host Academic Search Elite.

MLA style: Works Cited.

Typical book.
Last name, First name. *Book Title: Subtitle*. City of Publication: Publisher, Date.

Doe, Jane. *Understanding the Media: A Guide to Print and Broadcast Journalism*. New York: Deerlink Press, 2003.

Typical article.
Last name, First name. "Article Title." *Periodical Title* Volume (Year): Pages.

Doe, John. "Filtration Breakdowns and the Cigarette Butt Problem." *Water Treatment Monthly* 46 (2002): 221-227.

Typical Web page.
Last name, First name. "Article Title." *Web Site*. Date of Article. Sponsoring Organization. Date You Accessed Article <URL>.

Doe, Jane. "Kauai's Recent Hurricane Damage." *Vacations Unlimited*. 17 December 2002. Visitors and Vacation Travel Bureau of Kauai, Hawaii. 5 March 2004 <http://www.vacationinhawaii.com/kauai/hurricane.html>.

Note: Many Web pages do not contain all of the information described above. In such cases, include whatever information is available on the page. You may be able to locate the name of the Web site or the sponsoring organization by backing up to the root URL. In the fictitious example above, the root URL would be www.vacationinhawaii.com.

Typical database.
Last name, First name. "Article Title." *Periodical Title* Volume (Year): Pages. Database. Date You Accessed Article <URL>.

Doe, John. "Aristotle on Friendship." *Amicus* 32 (1999): 324-31. JSTOR. 4 November 2003 <http://www.jstor.org>.

Note: For articles in some electronic databases and some Web sites, the URL can become very lengthy. In such cases, use the root URL, as in the example above.

For further reference.

American Psychological Association. (2001). *Publication manual of the American Psychological Association* (5th ed.). Washington, D. C.: Author.

Gibaldi, J. (2003). *MLA handbook for writers of research papers* (6th ed.). New York: Modern Language Association of America.

References

Note: The sources attributed to John Doe, Jane Doe, Smith, and Jones are all fictional, as are those referencing the Lighting Institute, the Tapwater Beverage Company, and the examples in Appendix B. The following list covers the actual sources referenced in the text.

Harris, R. (2002). *Creative problem solving: A step-by-step approach.* Glendale, CA: Pyrczak Publishing.

International dictionary of psychology. (1995). New York: Crossroad.

Maheu, M. & Gordon, B. (2000). Counseling and therapy on the Internet. *Professional Psychology: Research and Practice, 31,* 484-489.

Nickerson, R. (1999). How we know—and sometimes misjudge—what others know: Imputing one's own knowledge to others. *Psychological Bulletin, 125,* 737-759.

Reynolds, J. (1797/1965). *Discourses on art.* Indianapolis: Bobbs-Merrill.

U. S. State Department. (2000, April 20). Travel warnings & consular information sheets. Retrieved February 10, 2001 from the World Wide Web: http://www.travel.state.gov/travel_warnings.html

Index

Notes

Notes

Notes

Notes

Notes

Notes